In the Green Mountains
By Shianne Dishroon

Dedicated to my supportive family.

You are my home base.

I yearn for my feet in the soil,
On the rock.
I want to touch every grain of sand and stone.
I need the salty air in my mane
So I can taste it when
It whips me in the face.
I crave the warm sun on my eyelids and
Hugging my shoulder tops.

    But most of all, trees!

Trees, which are the perfect blend of
Air dancing
Water-nourishing
Earthen rooted.

They go out of this life sacrificing themselves
To burn in fire & dissolve back into the ether of this world.

    I love you, wondrous nature
    Always a compass to me.

-quarantine day 50

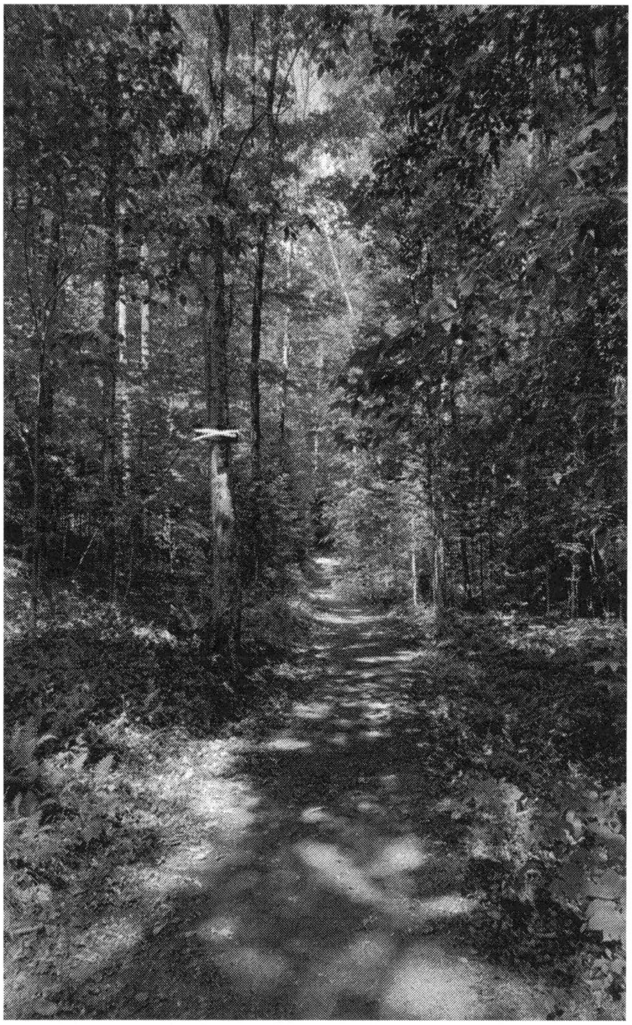

In the dark morning before the world wakes
I'm already on the road
Everything peaceful and clean
Anything possible and clear
The pace of the world slowed
While my wheels raced faster

How I love to feel the wind in my hair
On my face
Through my fingers
Interlinked on the wheel

Observing every place
And every way
In which others choose to live.

-*she's roaming*

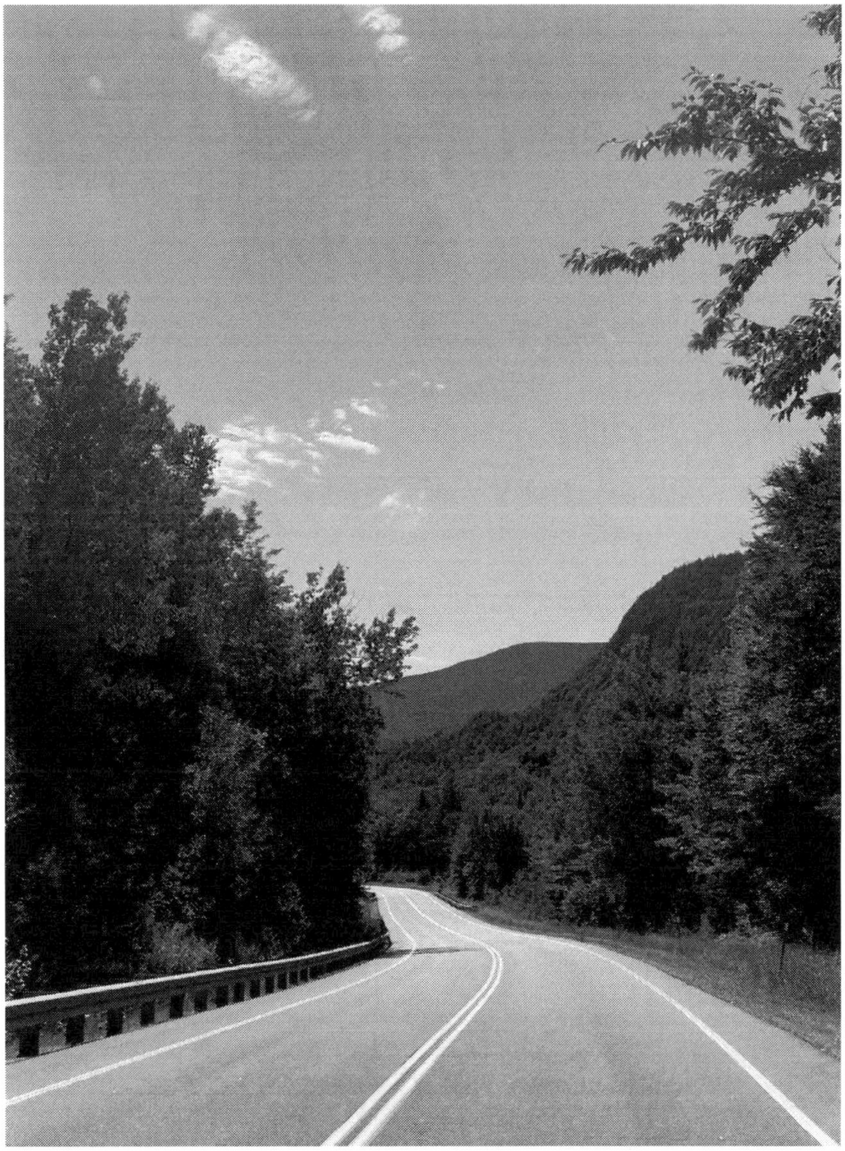

Today I woke up
And decided
Unapologetically
I am showing up to be my sole advocate.

I present myself with integrity
Courage.
Honor.
Gumption.
Offering all my values on display:
A feast for your searching eyes.

I trust my instincts will guide the way:
Creator
Destroyer
Chaos
Order

I refuse to die with my dreams,
I choose to expire with memories instead.

-a leap

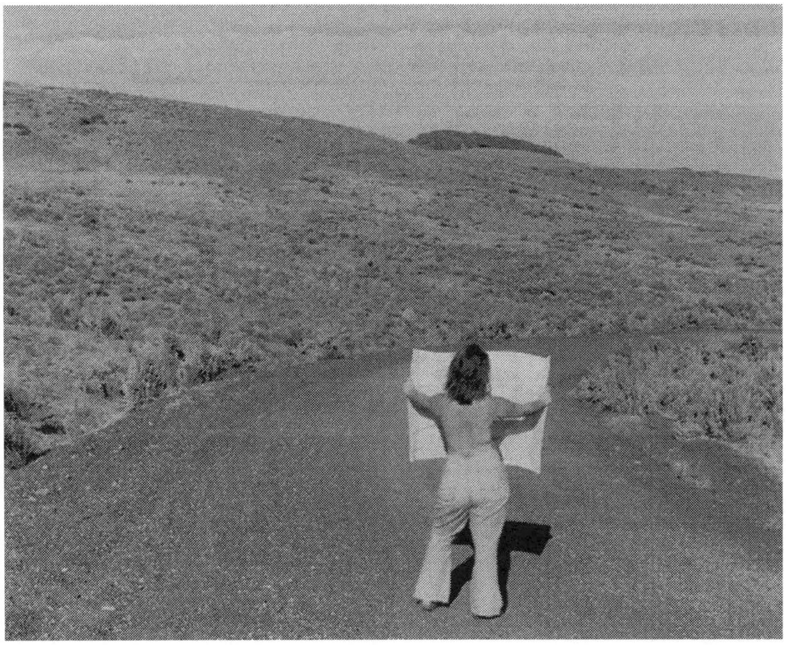

So many people
(that love me)
Thought that I couldn't, shouldn't

Cant.

And they were all shocked
When I went ahead

& did.

I never take offense about their superficial sentiments.

I like that
ELECTRIC FEELING
Of changing their perception!

My trip isn't about
Running away from life
It's about my sprinting towards it.

-living outside of the box we put me in

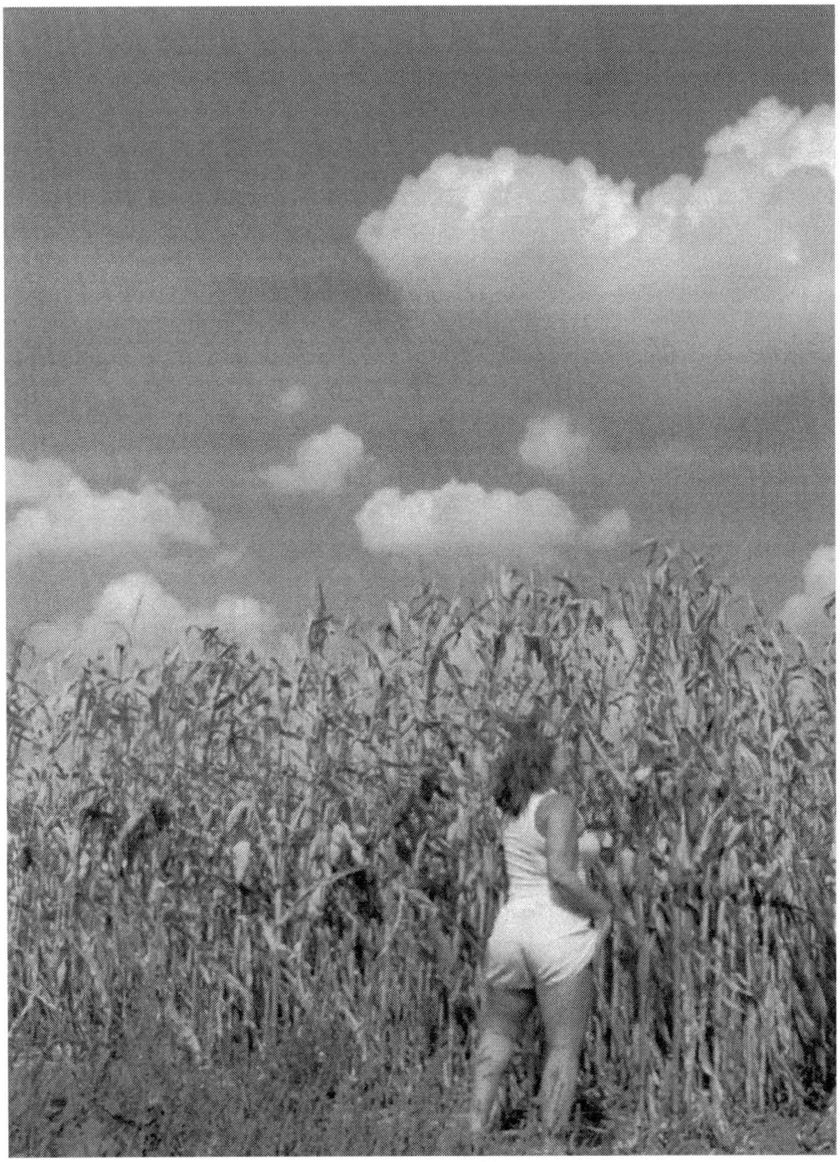

I am your harbinger
Of freedom
I show you how to
Liberate yourself

    You watch my grace in awe.

-*she's flying*

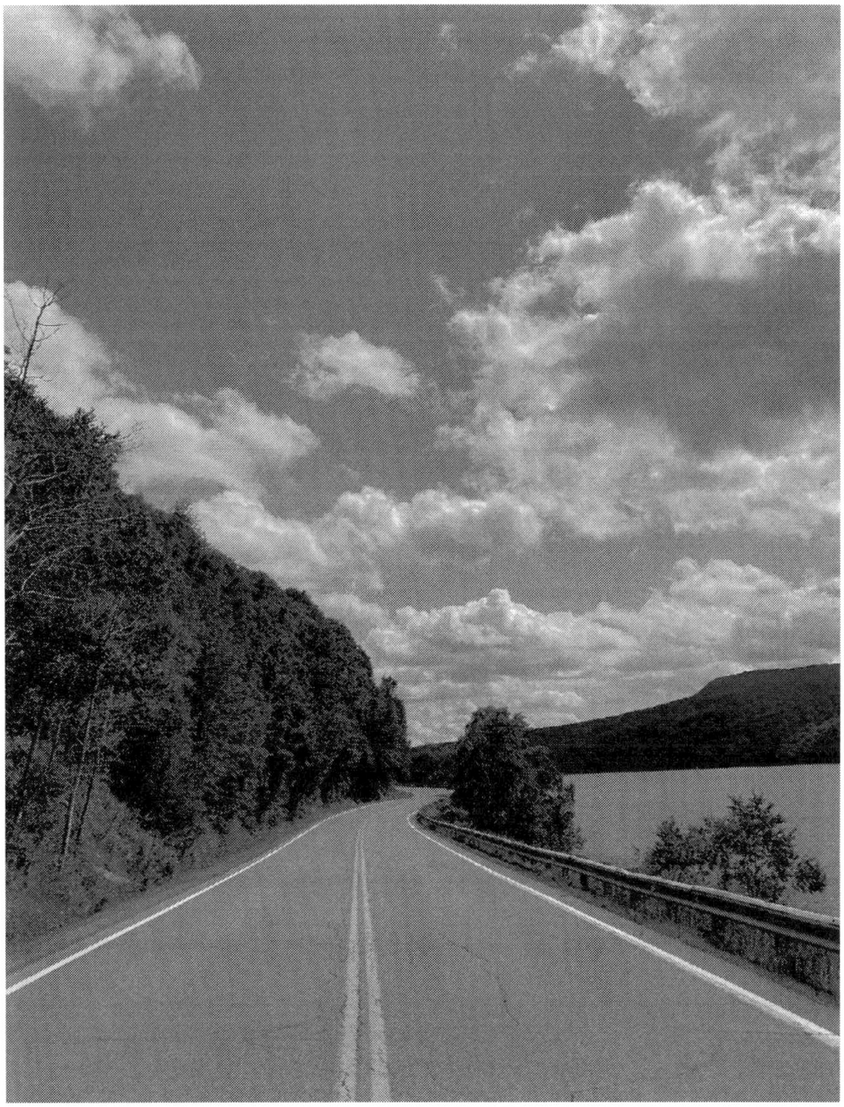

While life
Has been easier
On me
Being alone & unpartnered
All these years

I think now I gather
That I am ready to be in love.

Unsoundly in love with all that life wants to offer.

-a woman that's ready

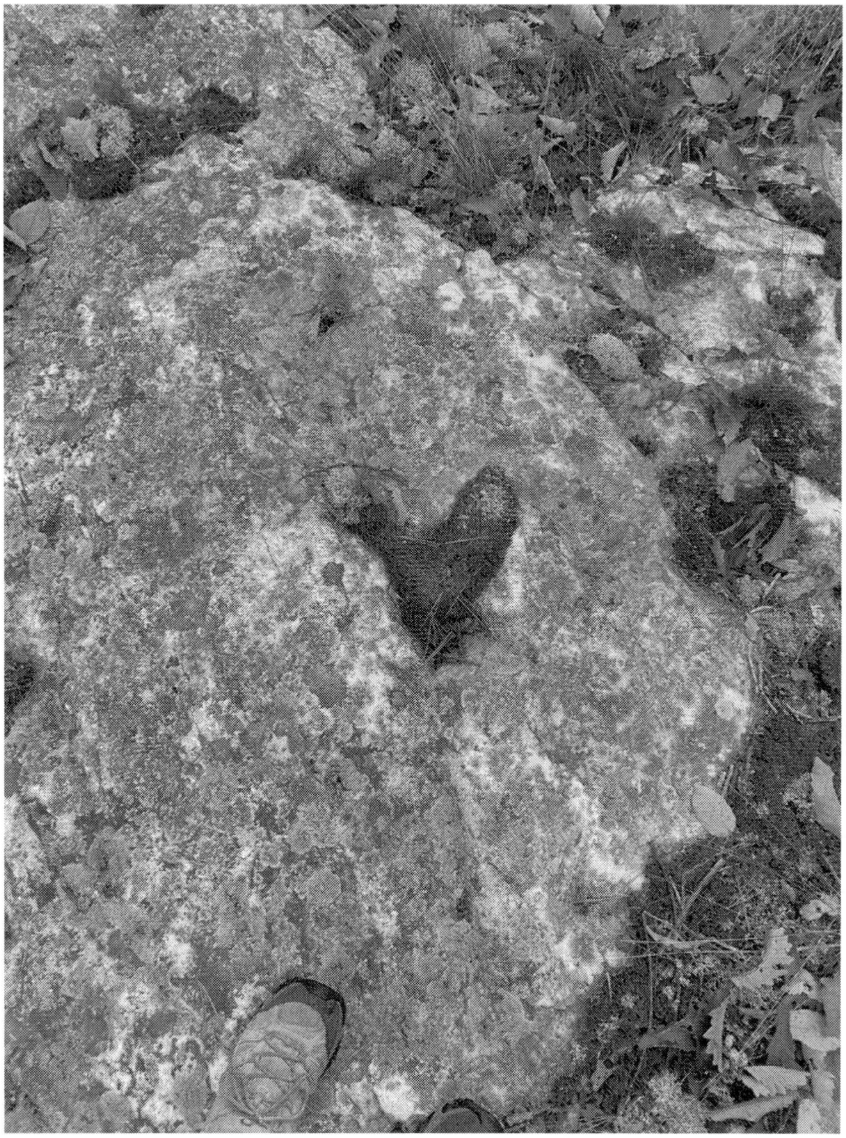

Old cupboards clanking from the kitchen
Charlie barking up a storm.
Be sure to take off your garden boots, at the door.

And always stoop down to pet the cat.

Dusty books are stacked along the shelves
Some are signed or written in foreign tongues.
Homemade maple syrup is always for sale
A family recipe passed down through the trees.

-this is home, for now

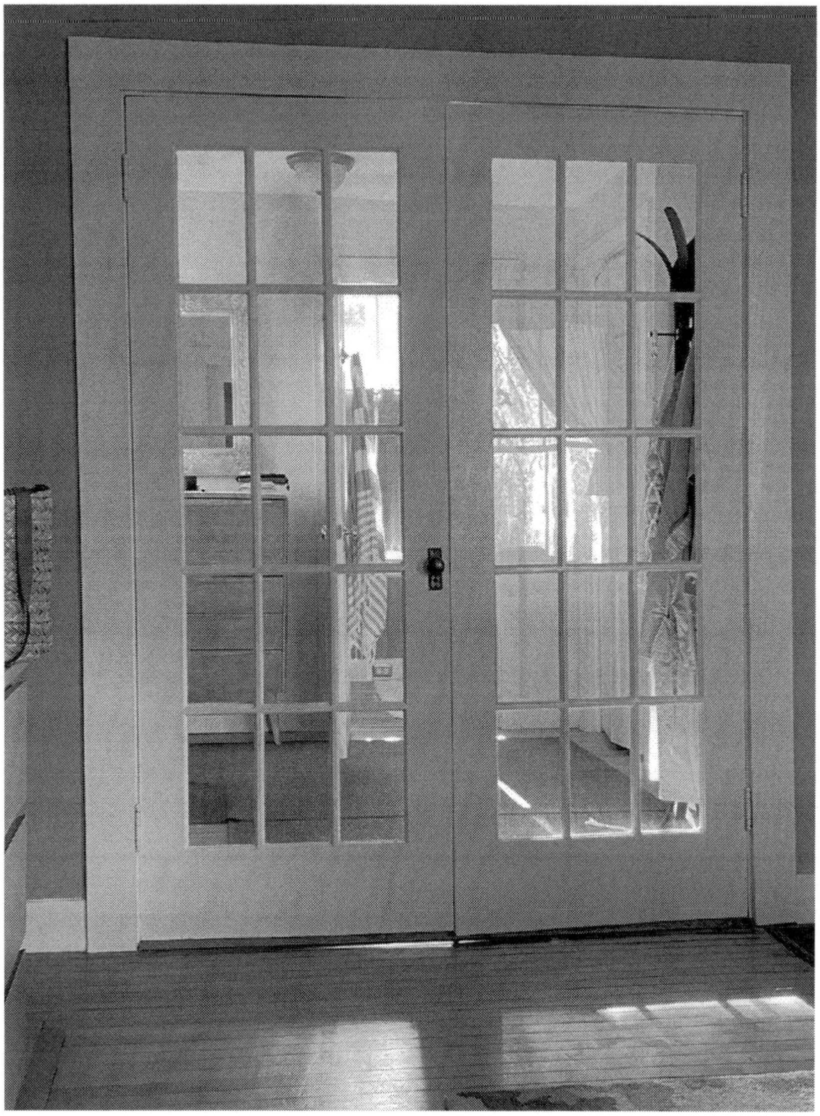

Tigerlillies bloom wild
Here in Vermont.

    (Just like me!)

    That's one of the signs I knew I belonged.

-a blossoming

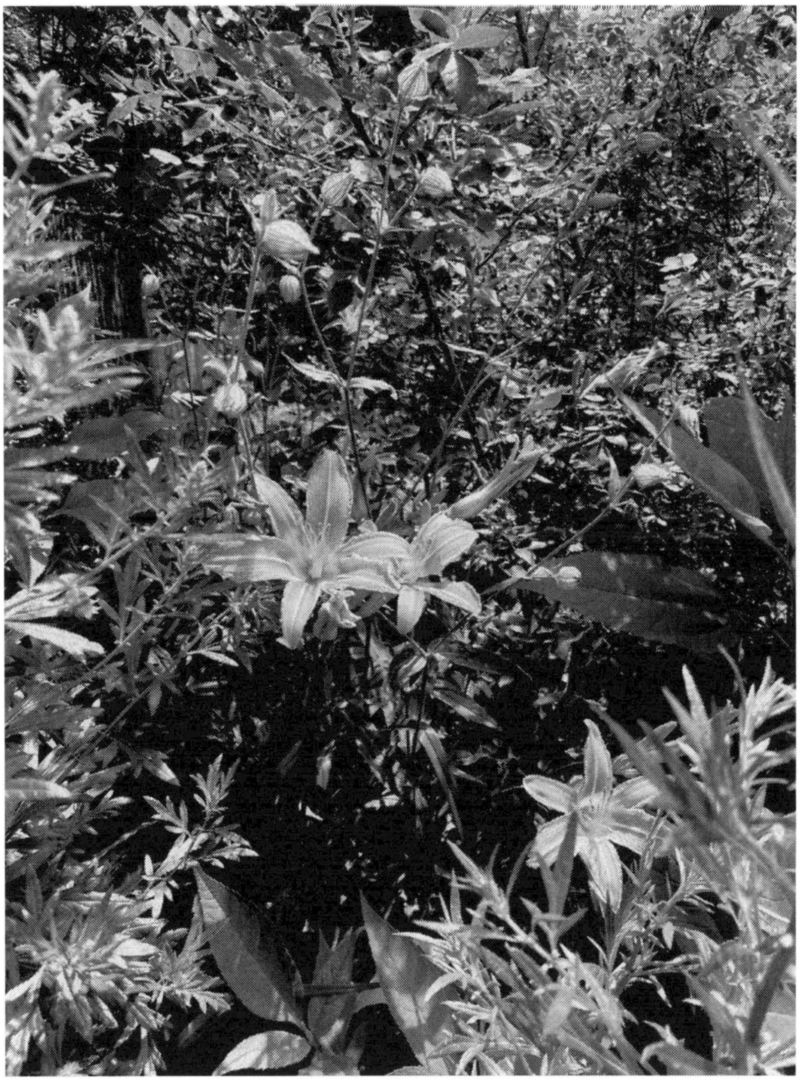

A quiet space
A gentle time just for me
I have my face mask on
I have my hot tea

There is a sound of running bath water
There is a notebook for my thoughts
Just me and Time and God in this room
The perfect place to be

-an Artemis afternoon

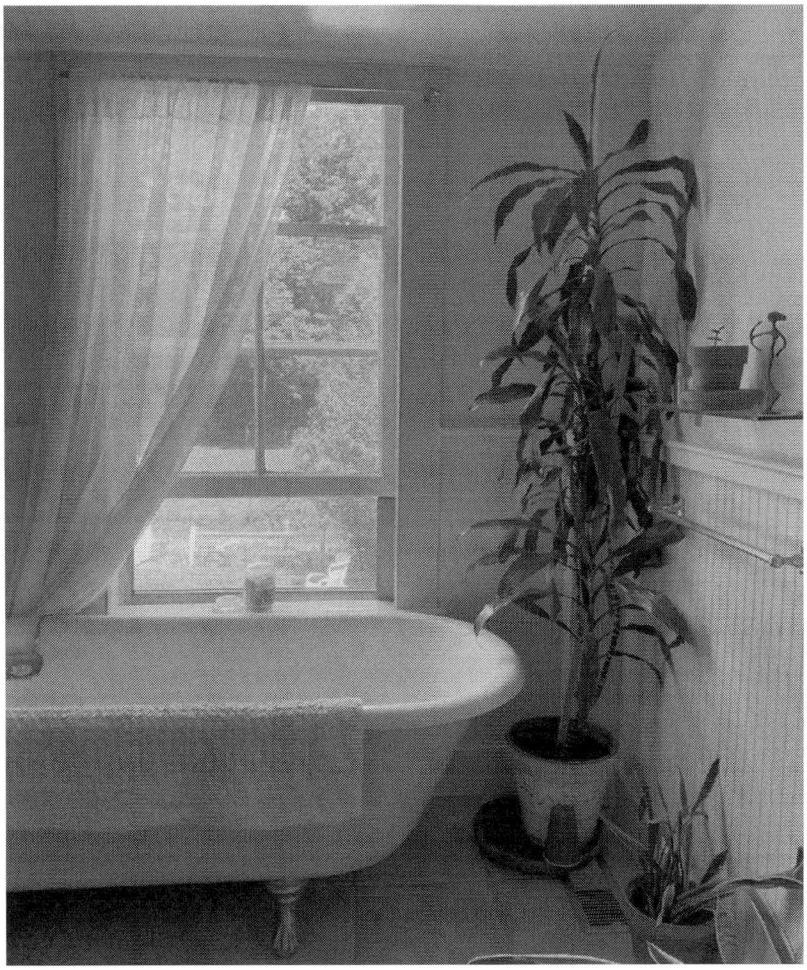

When his girlfriend was out of town-
When the farmhand he liked wasn't looking-
A drunken fool came to my door and tried to sneak a kiss

The frogs this season were very loud
All full of ego and demanding
For every want and need

But I played it cool
I wouldn't be cruel
To all those frog fools in heat.

-kissing boys

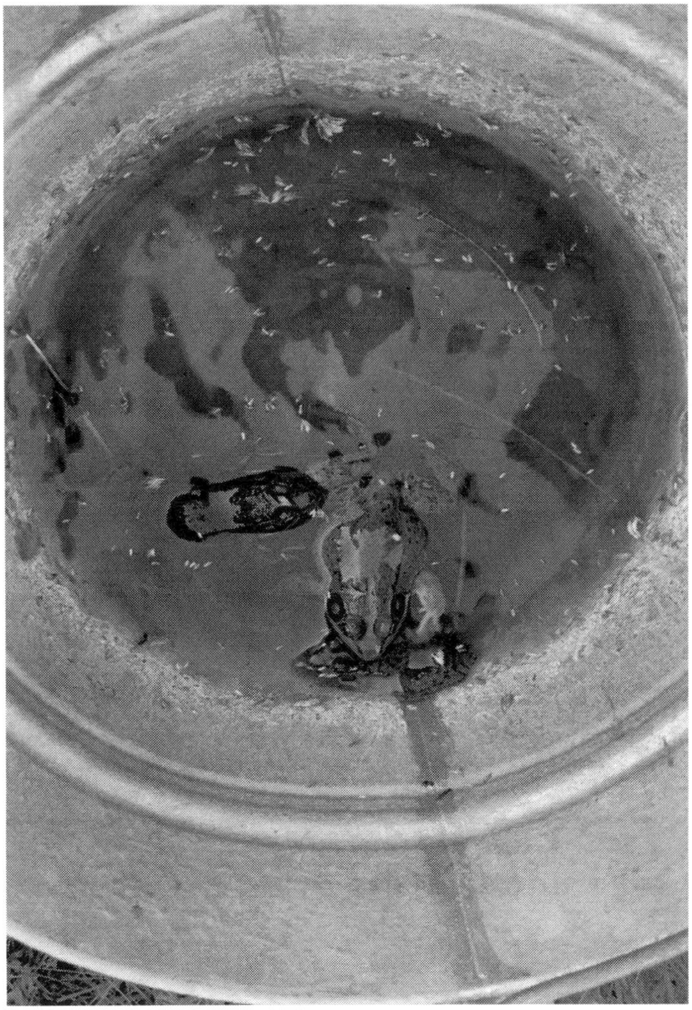

I need to stand before
Vast lands often
To feel insignificant and small
It gives me courage to meet my life
Where I need to be.
Who I should become.
How I want to live.

-infinite and healing places

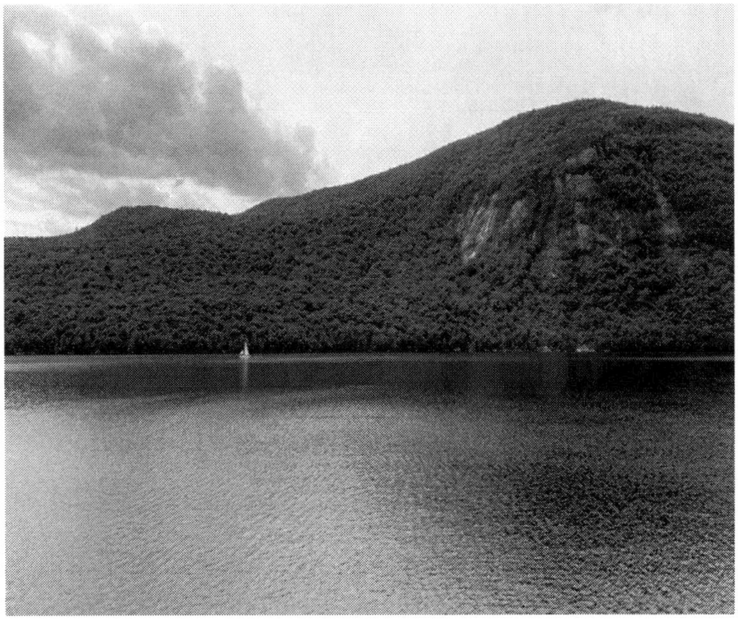

Winding through hills
And mountain roads
Past church and steeple
Admiring the clouds, skipping in the treetops

Isn't it something to think
That at one point
You come into a small town

Where the man you care for lives
(hidden among the stone wall, hill and tree)

And you think to yourself:

    This place has everything I need.
    A place to keep my heart.

-Winooski

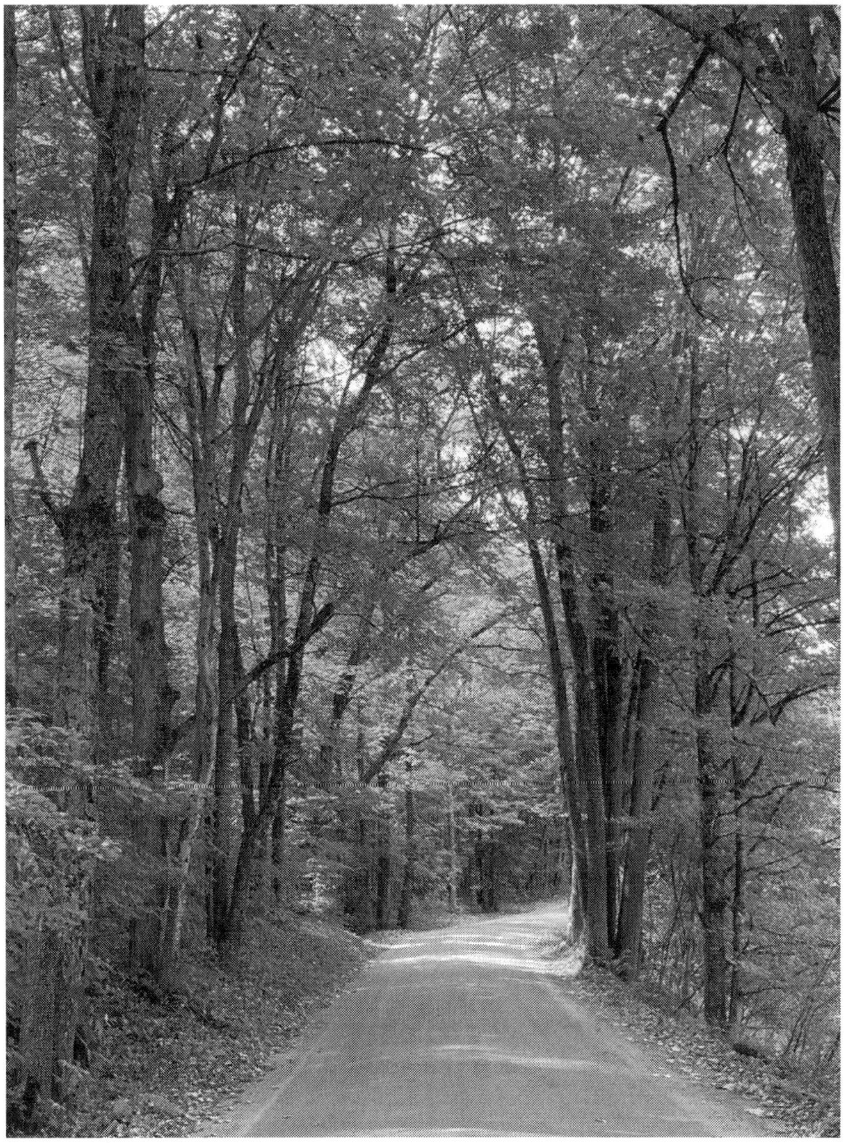

Take time, dear Leslie
I know you're working well into your seventies
Don't be a miser, come sit
And admire
All the beauty you have grown

The lives you have saved!
From farm newt, alpaca, and apple tree
Little lives revised

All of us passerby's living here
Including me

-reap the benefits

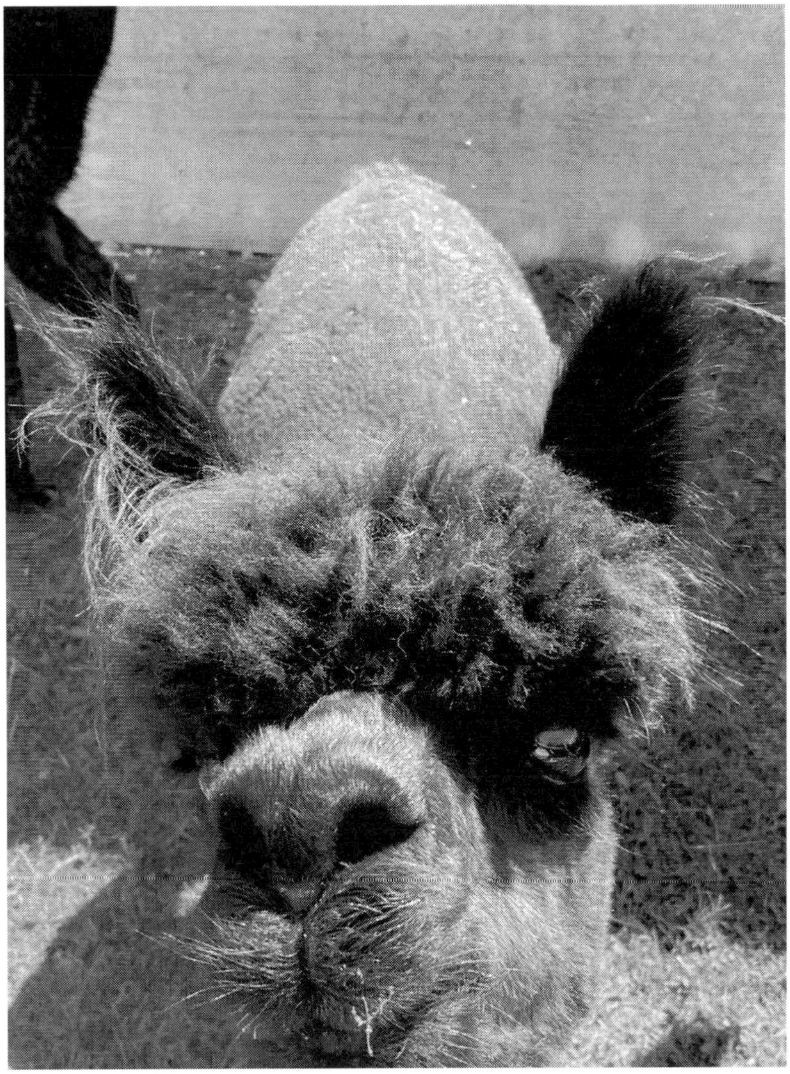

The darkness on the East Coast
Lately has been depressing me

Being from California
I'm unsure I'll last in this murky place.
Normally each morning
The sun awakens my iridescent spirit.

This here is entirely new.
I'm trying to embrace the gloomy chill.
Holding out for the dream I've had
Of an east side summer-

Topless drives
Bonfires
A good man to love
Green trees tall around me

Yet each day here without the sun my inner flame smolders.
I'm afraid one day I will be as ashen as this sky.

-sunbeam's quandary

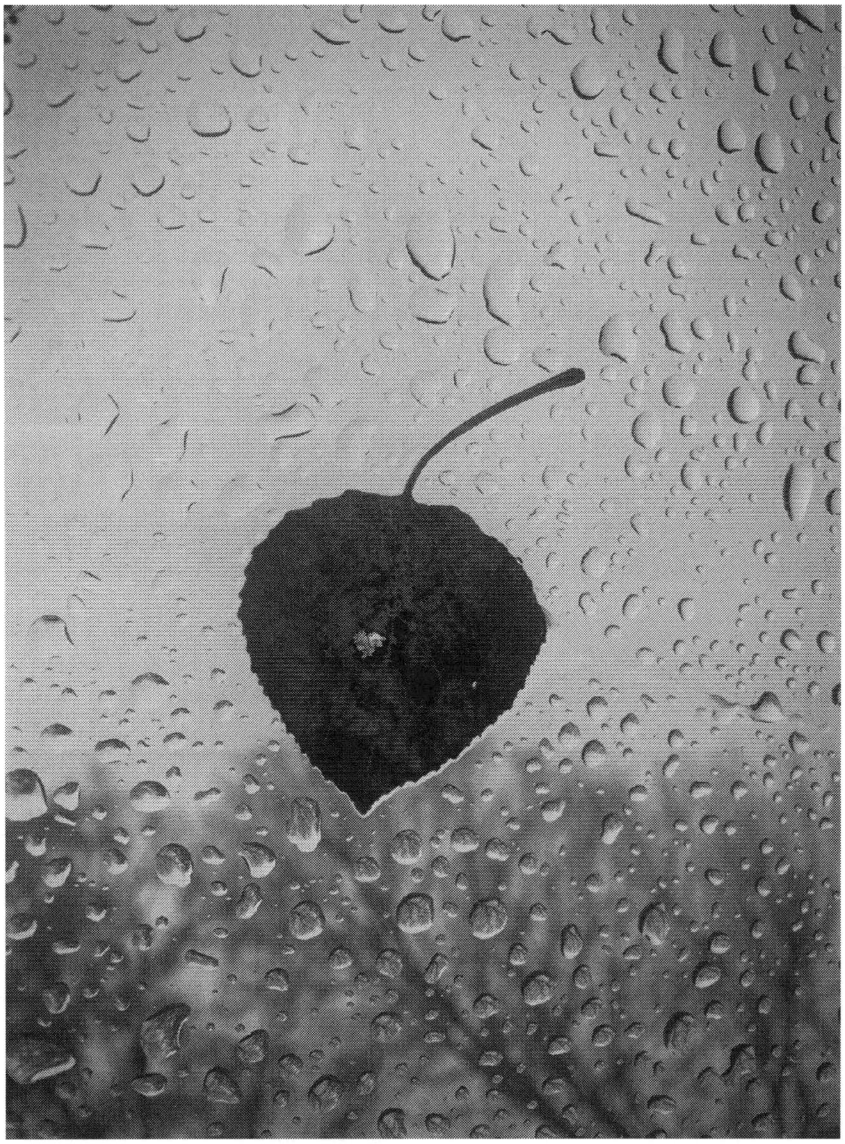

Tonight, my aching heart was ablaze
Within the campfire

Healing &
Sewn back together
With the leaves of wild ferns

Patched with bark from a birch tree
Threaded with poplar and pine

The chilled waters
Washed me of my feelings
And baptized me here
In this earthly haven

Misty mountains mending me

-some kind of phoenix

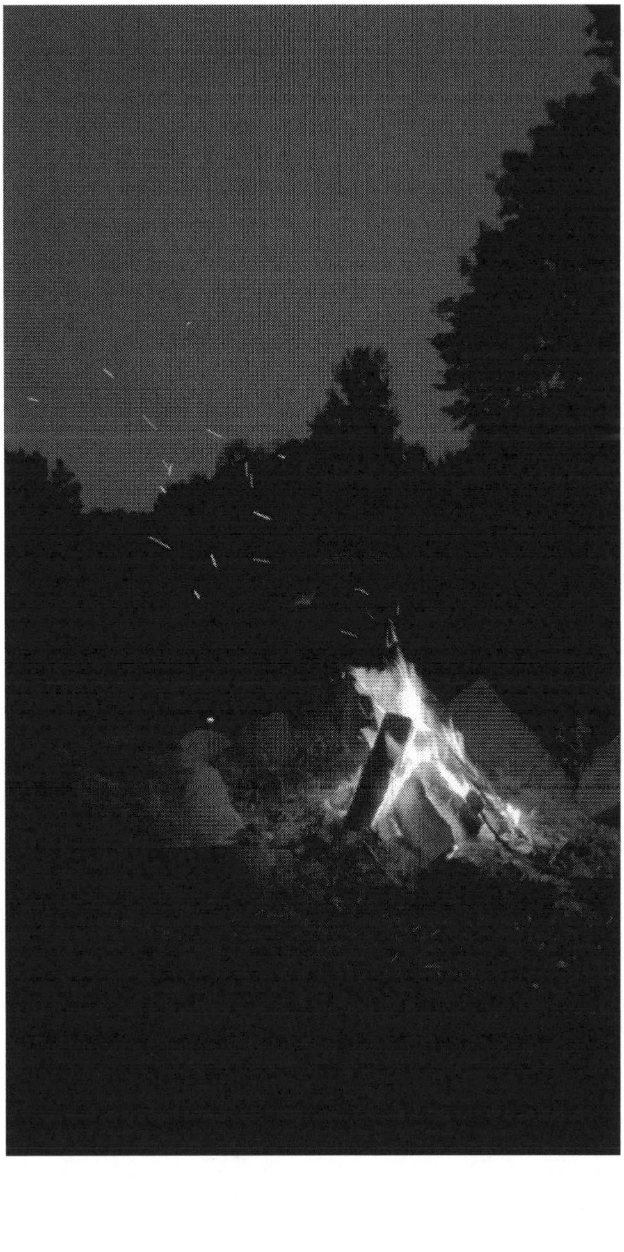

Most early mornings this summer
Ole Sally & I
Have coffee out by the pool
Near the fragrant sea roses

Dainty pink petals basking in the sun
Honeybees diligently gathering their plenty

I sip my decaf with half & half
While Sal sits further back away
And has a smoke.
We stay in comfortable silence.

I rise to do a gentle yoga stretch,
Or meditate on the diving board
Arms and feet dangling
Dipping my toes in
The bright aqua water

This is a staple for me
Friendship on the farm.

-a good morning

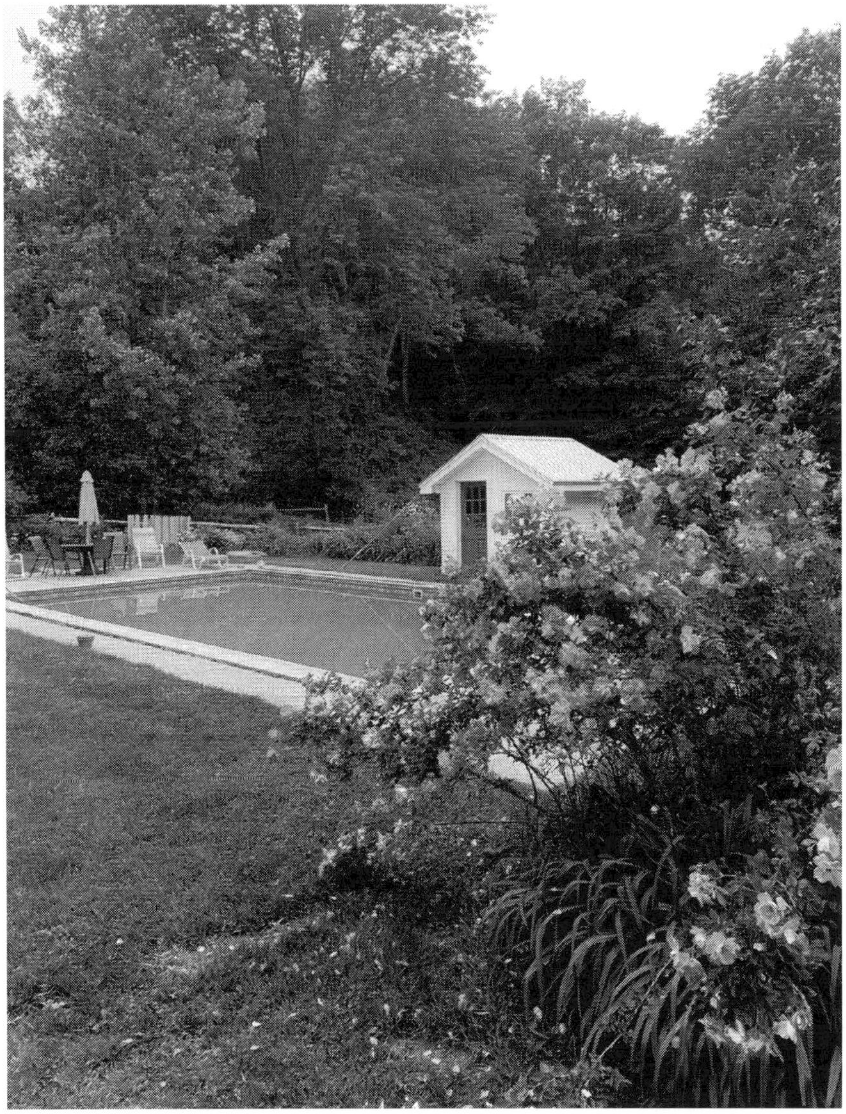

I spend afternoons down at the river
Among ladybugs, butterflies, and beavers

Each morning, I go to the small, local shack
And pick up seasonal fruit and co-op cheese
Sometimes a blueberry wine

With my headphones on, I lay on some stone
And daydream the hours away
In between dips or laps upstream

-my secret riverbend

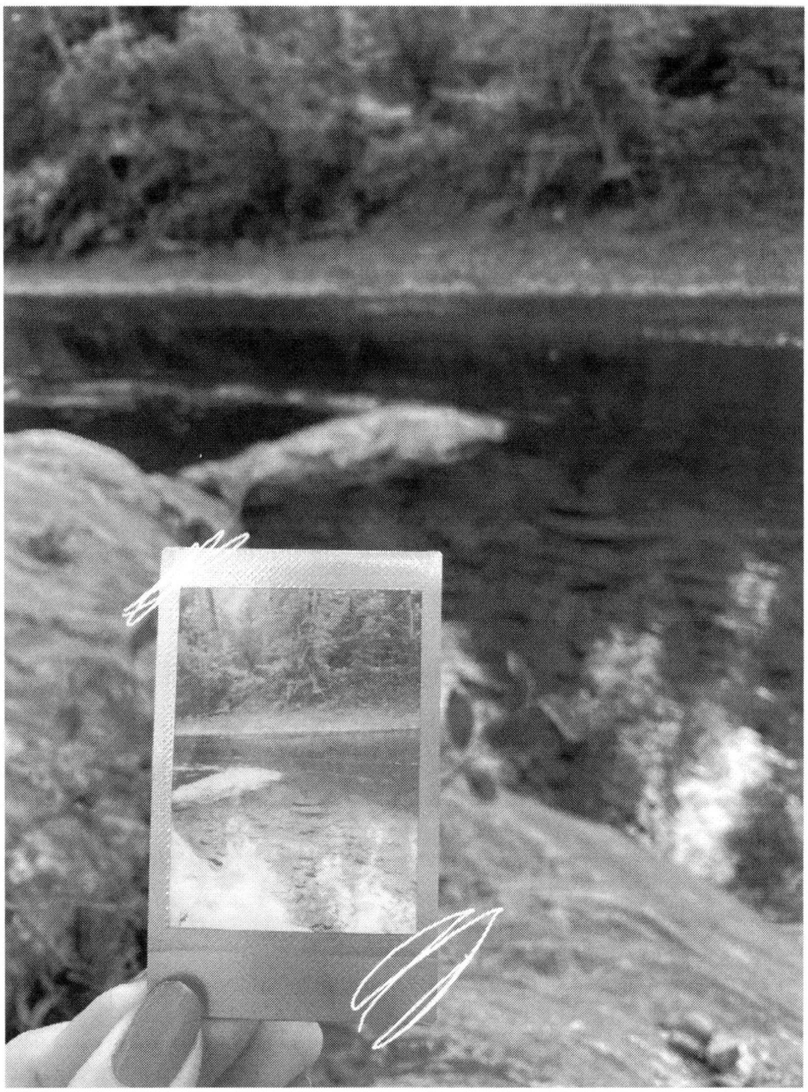

I'm too much for most people.

Especially men.

Intensely passionate.
Deliciously erotic.

Hot, sweeping, mouth melting
Heart-on-fire loving
A blazing woman
Able to harness
Her Cosmic Wilderness.

I consume adventure for dessert each day
I bellow for any wrongdoing in this world
& laugh at myself in between

My honey-soaked alluring energy attracts them

Yet I have not met a man
That would indulge
In such richness

Every day.

-a kind of cake

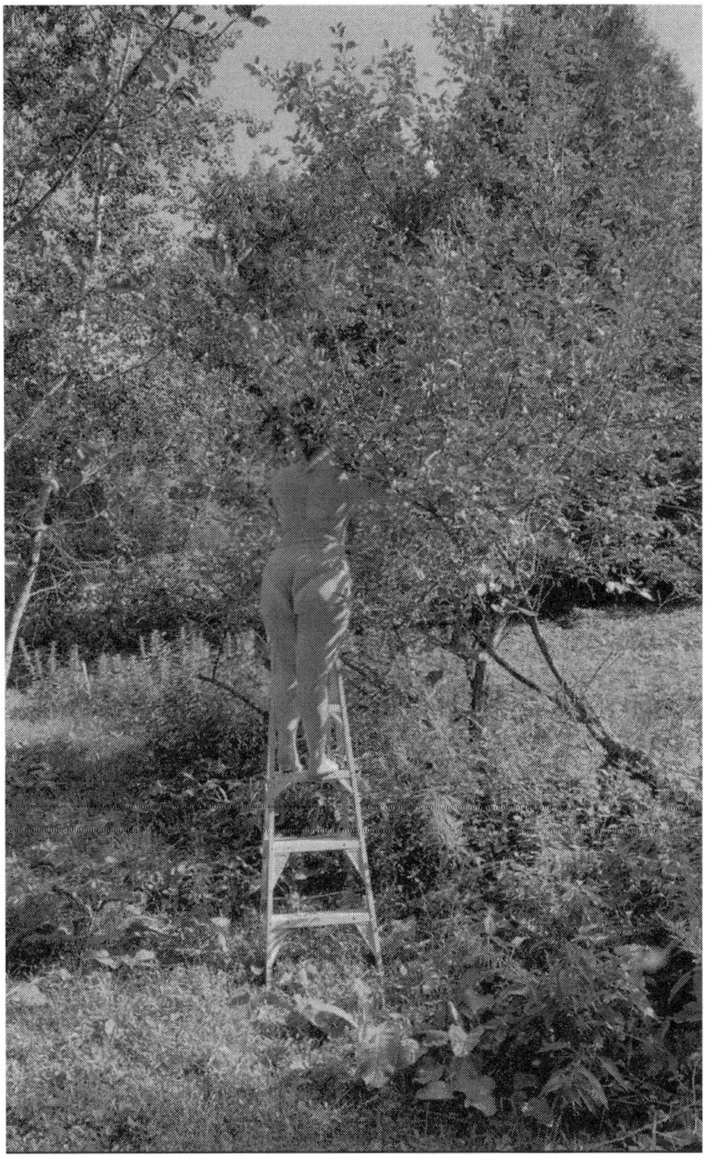

She stayed in bed a year
After her husband had passed
And now she spends her days
Listening to his songs
And volunteering to prune the lawn
Of his family's old estate
To feel closer to the soil he played on as a child
To the stems of trees and pink roses
That grew tall and bloomed around him as a youth

I wish we all her kind of strength and beauty
And appreciation for small things
And memory

-loving Annie

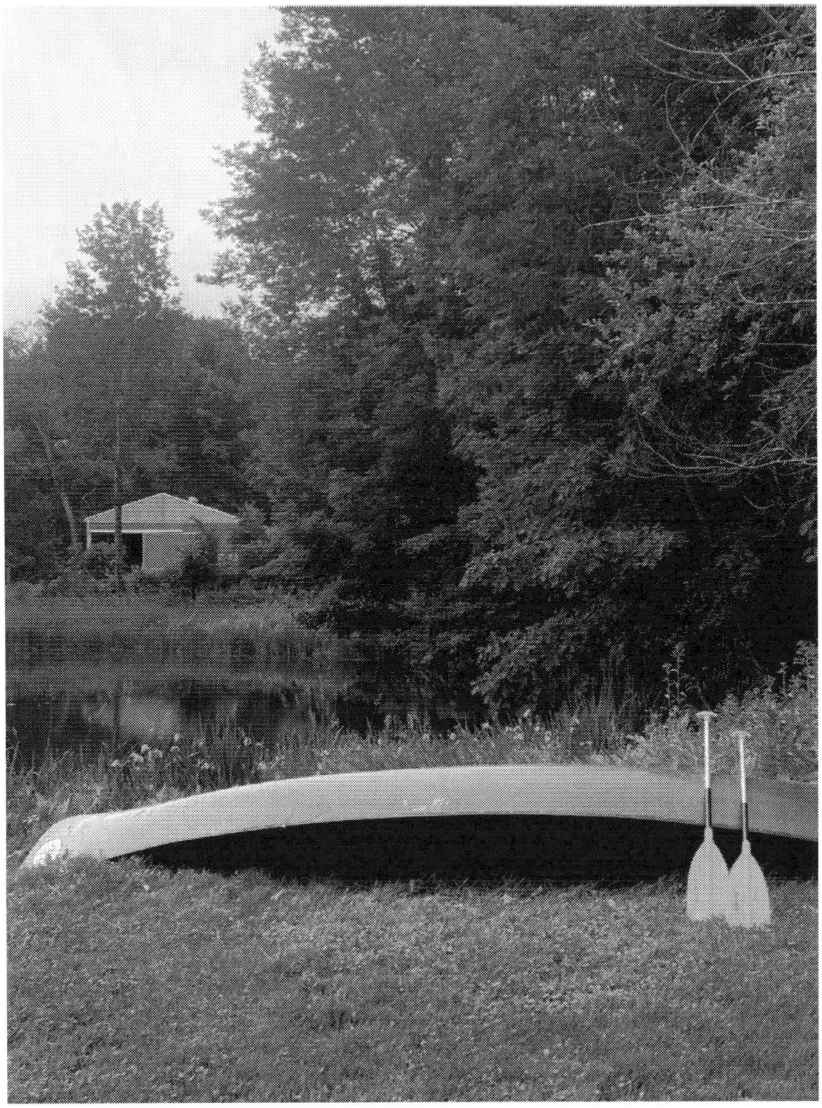

He called me up to say
He was driving from Cali
Back home to Vermont
"We can eat rabbit and swim in the river"

I sat and watched the flowers you picked
They had dried up
All the petals fallen-
This wasn't going to work out

-it wasn't for me

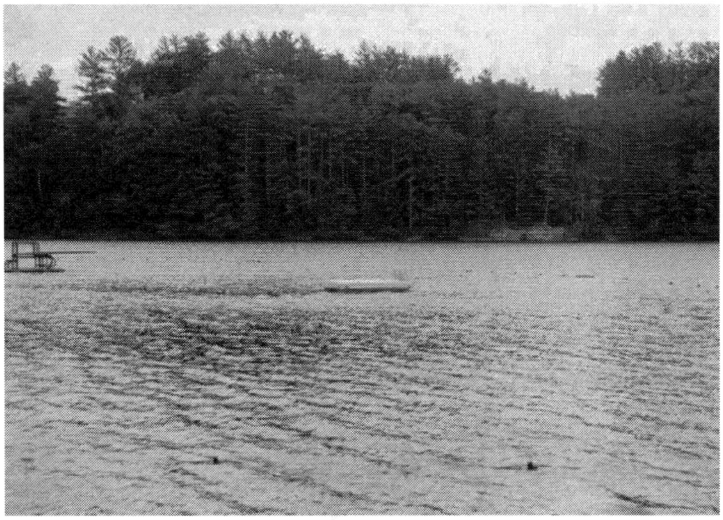

Nature interacts with me Here
More than any other Where I've been:

A chipmunk
Runs out of its hiding place
While I'm swimming
To graze on the wild blackberries
Near the pool.

A grasshopper
Flying higher than I've seen one rise
Comes circling my head
Over and over
Each time I'm near the
Fresh water spring, among the fern gully.

I've dreamt of a
Secret Garden like this all my life.

-childhood dreams come true

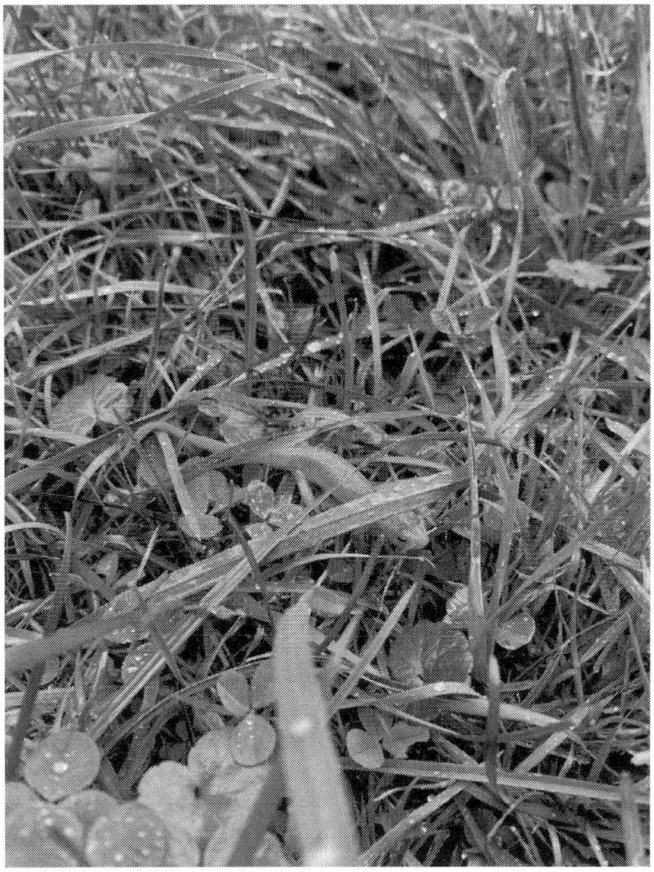

He picked me up
At the end of the gravel road

Outside the barn
The alpacas watched me
My blue dress on

Riding around with him was such
A joy for me
He showed off
      (His world)
& the beauty that surrounded us

My heart had already fallen

We swam in the
White river
With nothing on
But smiles

Watching the eagles
The beavers
& climbing rocks together

By the time we were back at my front porch
Kissing sweetly goodnight
I was glowing bright as the moon

-a first date

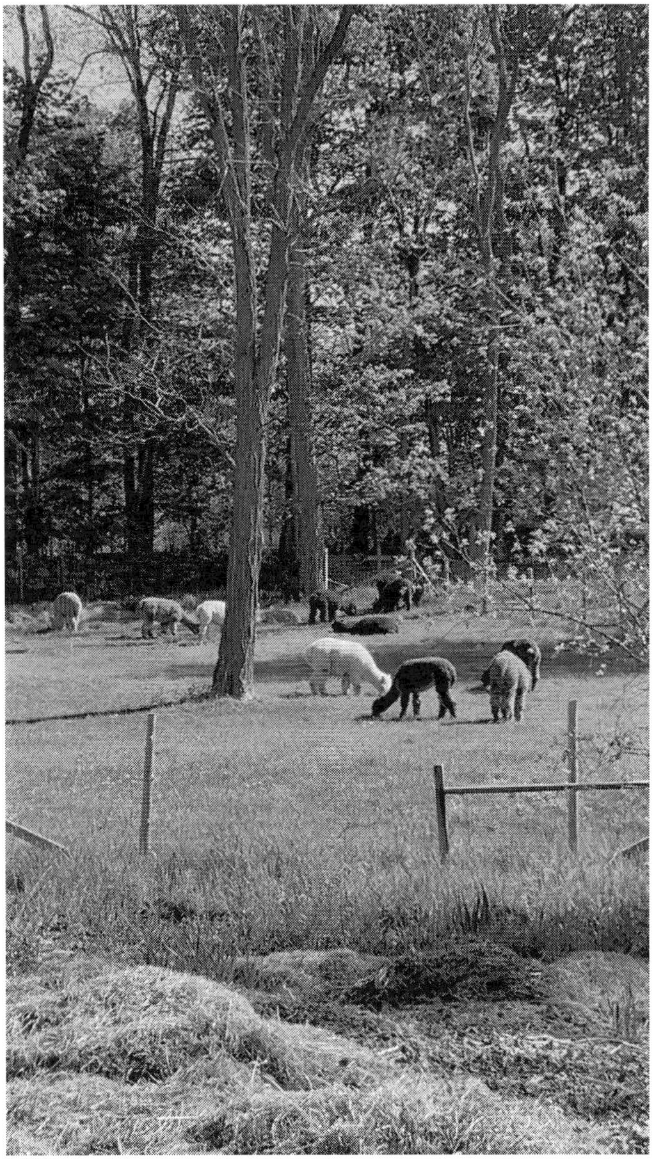

Sunshine shower on me
Rejuvenate each cell of my weary soul
Wash away the crumbling
Dead parts of myself
That have scabbed and need to fall away

Nature healing me
Soothing my spirit into something new
Purer and meant to be

-summer showers

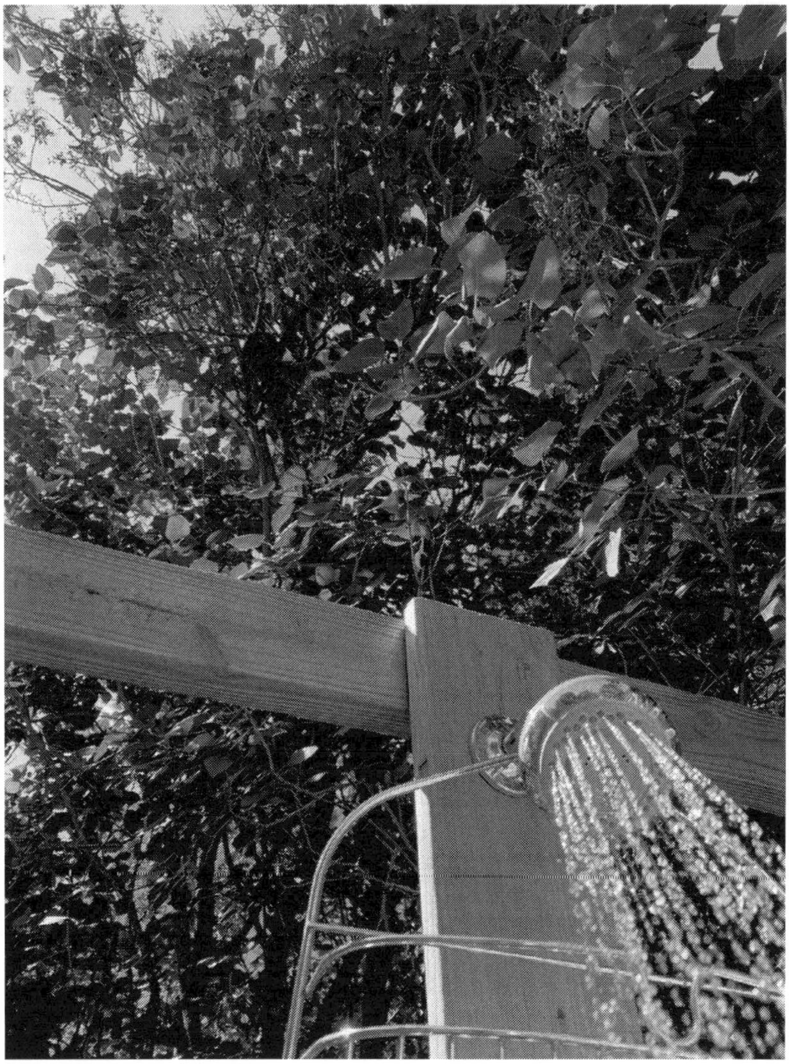

It hit me recently
My happiest moments were all in an instant of motion!

Physically:
Laughing
Swimming
Running
Smiling
& playing.

Not because of a partner's affections
Nor landing a big sale.
Unbased on a paycheck
Regardless of my car,
or home.
Not due to a graduation
Or landing a job.
Not one external, validating moment.

But rather during large swells of laughter,
My hair flying up & about,
Swaying in the wind.

The best part in those moments is
I was never alone.
It was shared with friends, family-
Community.

-in motion

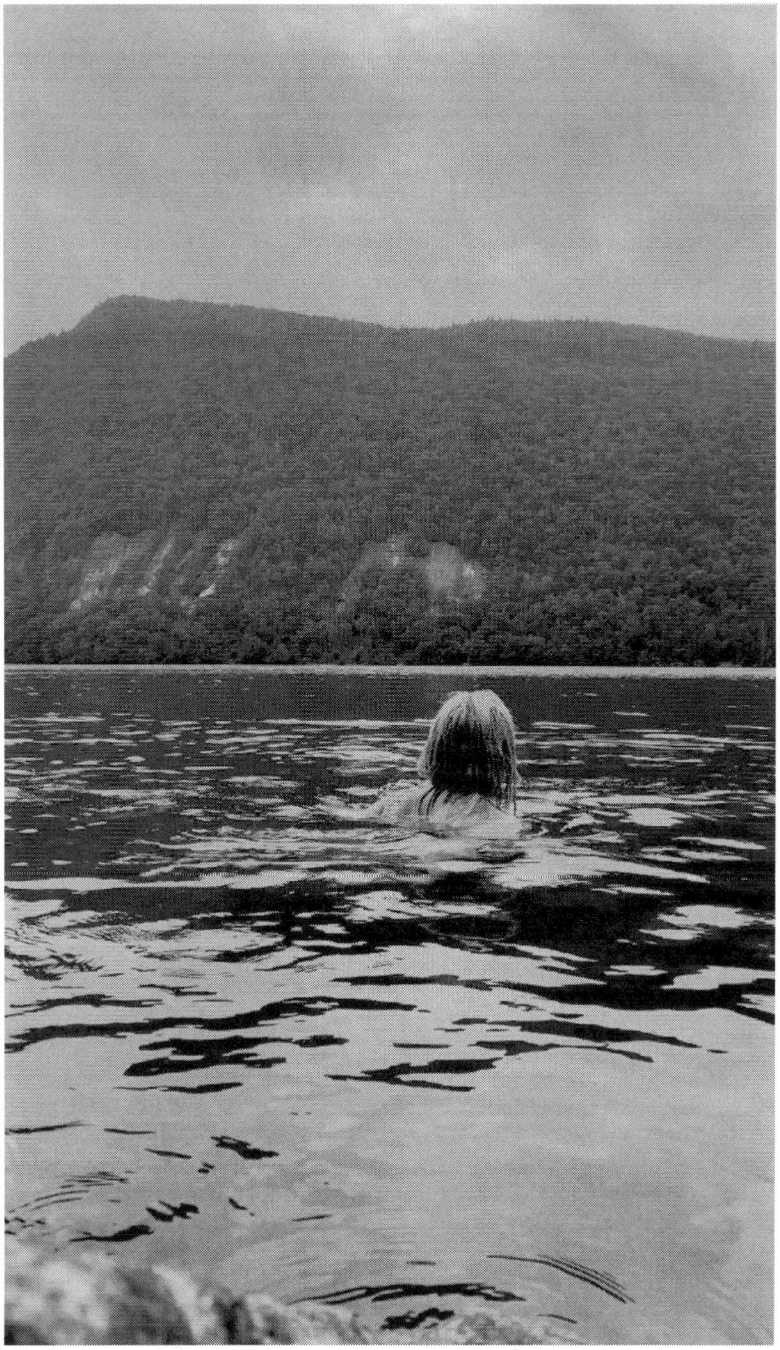

I play us some folk music at first
"Pink Moon" makes my heart swell

He stops and picks me wildflowers
Smiling as I watch, smelling the haystacks laid out to dry

He puts on old country western
Jimmy Dean, Willie Nelson
& then "Cowpoke" on repeat

We both love these drives together,
To our favorite place, or with Nowhere in mind.

We roll over every hill there is
Talking, holding hands, quick lustful looks.
I pretend to pout for his affections.
His humor is as cunning as the foxes along the roadside.
    (remember how I cried in surprise when we saw the babies?)

Miracles happen.
The local creatures come out of hiding when we're together.
The Universe exclaiming:
"You two wild animals are one of us!"

I wish we were those eagles, that day on the log.
Soaring above these woods together.

-a falling infatuation

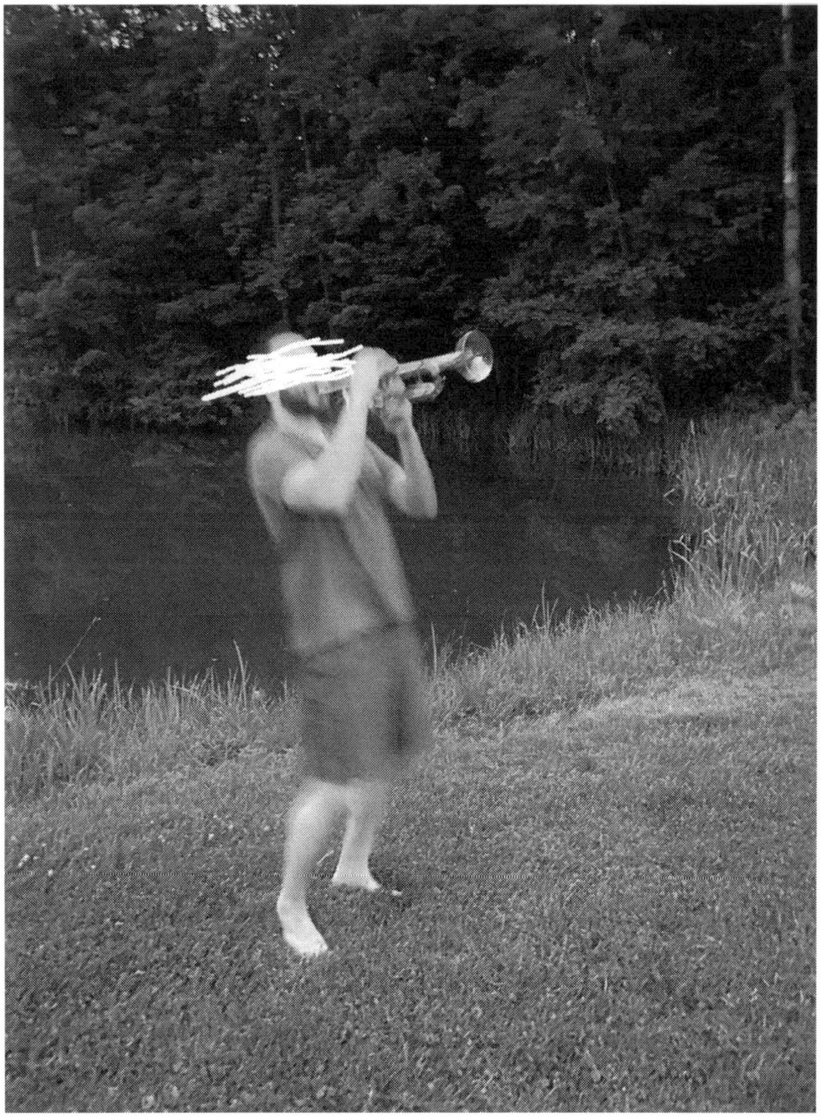

Freefalling is the goal in each of my days-
Power in my body, and confidence in my Self
I am discovering new doors and hidden aspects
I have been quiet but not here, not anymore
Who knew I had such an extroverted side?
That I could languidly sit in this body
Or flirt with unknown opportunities?
Not me.

I have found myself more kind here,
To myself and to others
More kind than I've been in places known to me.
Why is that?

I have run thousands of miles away and
Found an unleashed Me.
Now I frolic through grasses and sing boldly.
Meet me at the rope swing and I will show you.

-we can all play together still

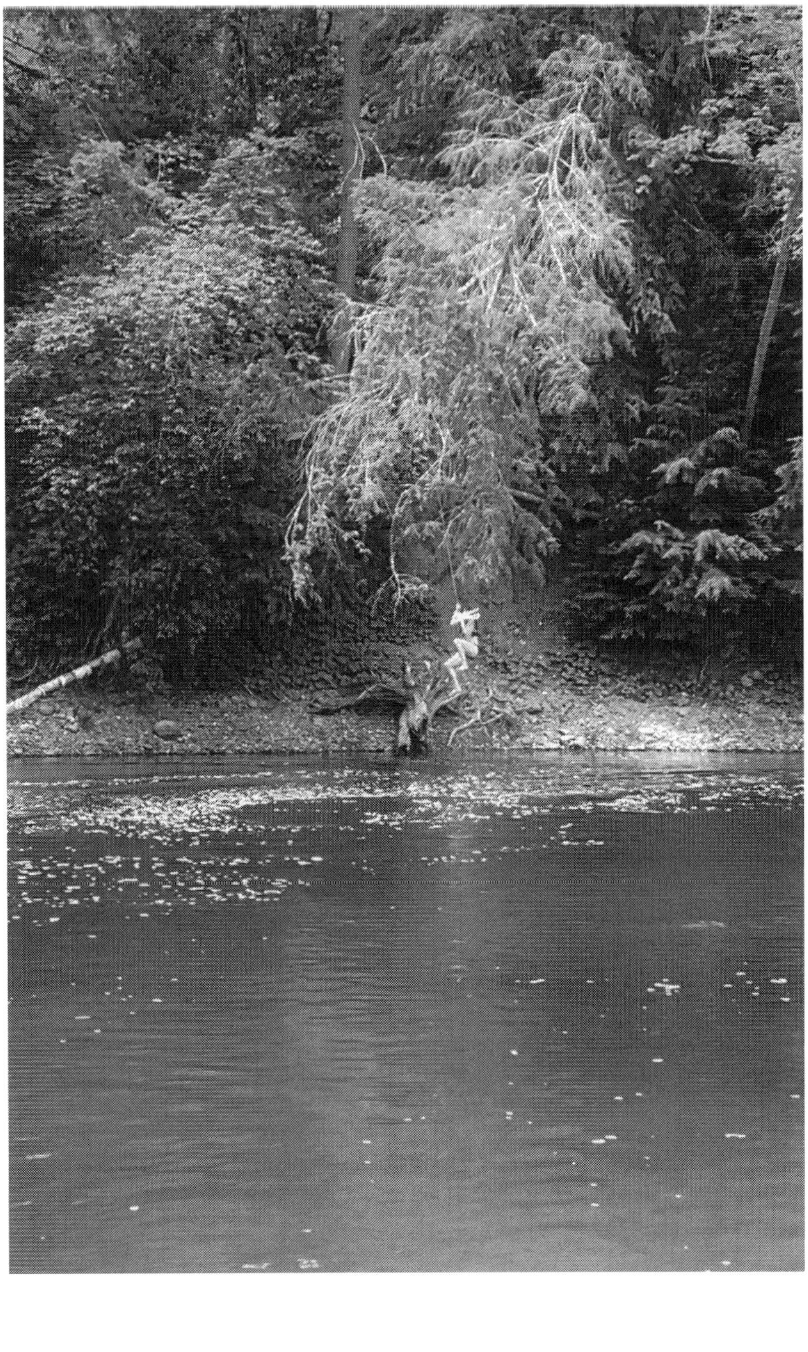

He was so lovely
Easter-blue eyes
Speckles of green like the trees he loved-
They would light up like a child's

Gentle hands, exquisite mind
A benevolent heart
A meek outward essence
Inside hiding a resilience, he didn't show.

I felt safe, then,
To be daring in new ways
(although he always called me the Wild One)

I'd trail behind him so long as he held my hand.

-that smile had me

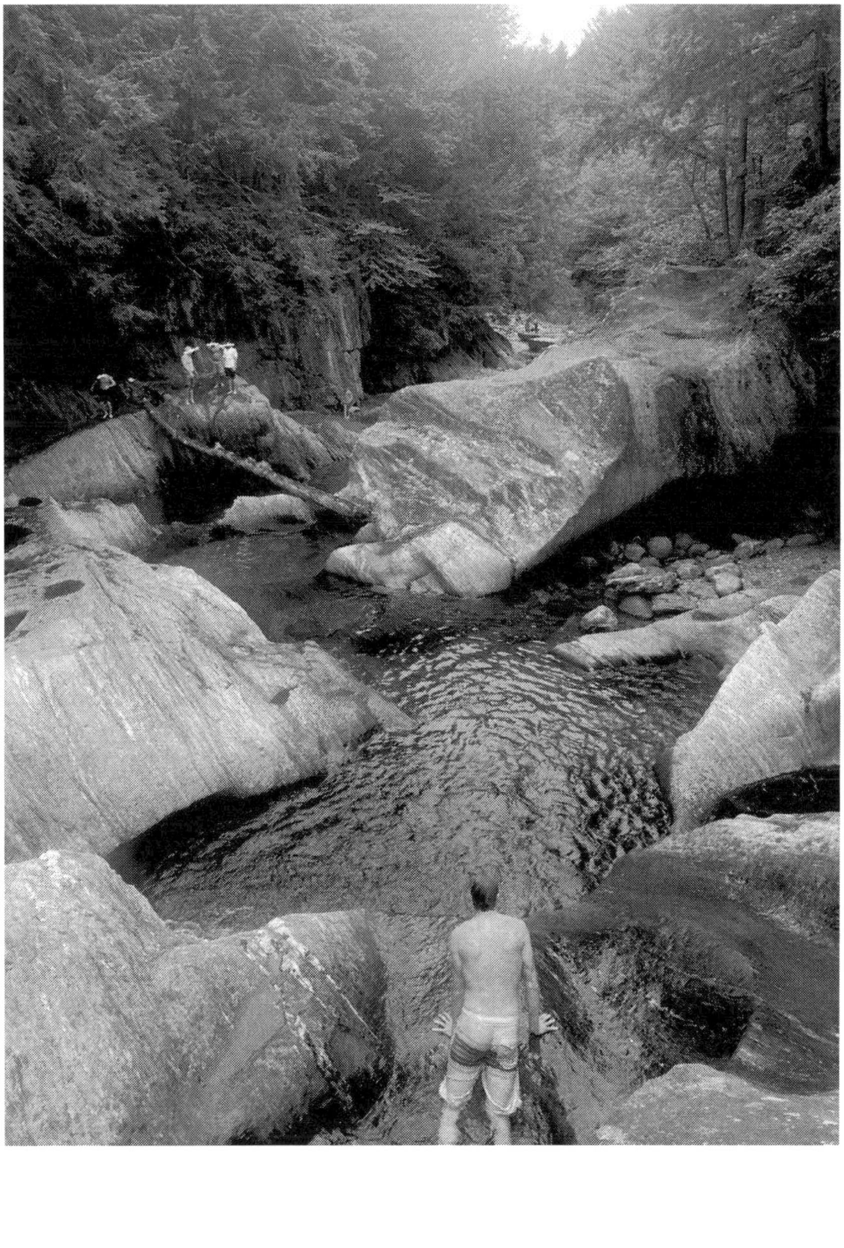

Do I watch the flowers grow?

Or are they watching me?

-a creator or an observer

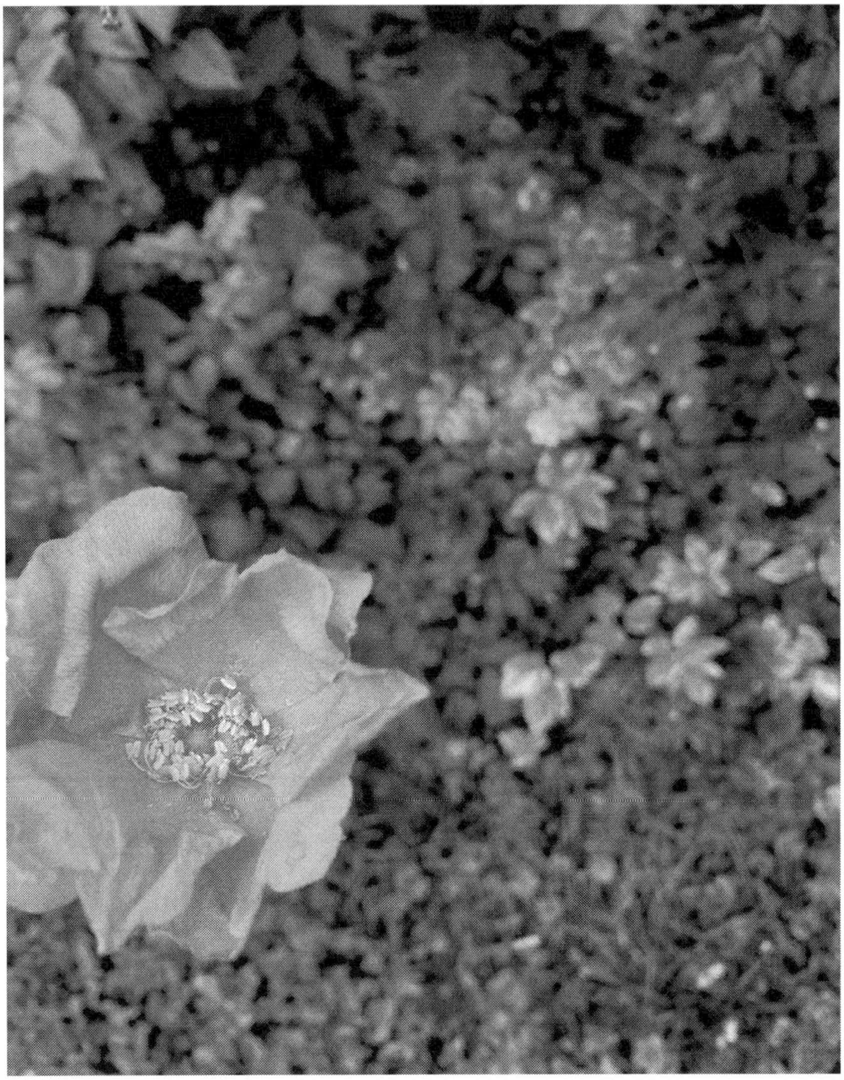

Tonight, I told him just
How handsome he is.
Vigorous, vulnerable,
Sympathetic
Stimulating & skillful
        (a Mountain) man.

I never suppress a generous thought- he knows this.

While looking away and up at the sky he said
"Don't love me,
        'Cause I'm a bad man," in a weak voice.

Without pause I traced his shoulder blade
And said resolutely "I know you're not."

He differed,
Unaware that I have seen what deranged men
Are capable of.

And while he wore a cloak of guilt and confusion
Tormenting himself
Indecisive and unsure

I could see through his threatening
And I knew he was lovely.

-the forewarning

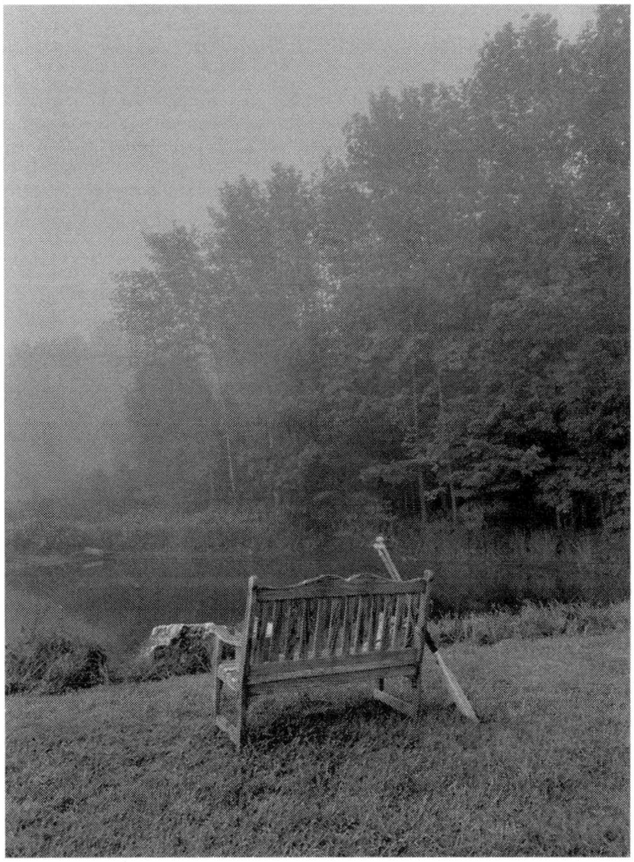

Mountainous medicine woman
Heal me with your tonics, your teas
My illness and ailments have burrowed a place inside me
That the doctor has cut out and cured

But I am weak after that catastrophe
I am weary after this long journey

There is a beginning of diaphragm breathing
There is a charge for stretching of the skin and muscle
Here is where the spark strikes
Here is the stirring I need to rouse

-apothecary journey

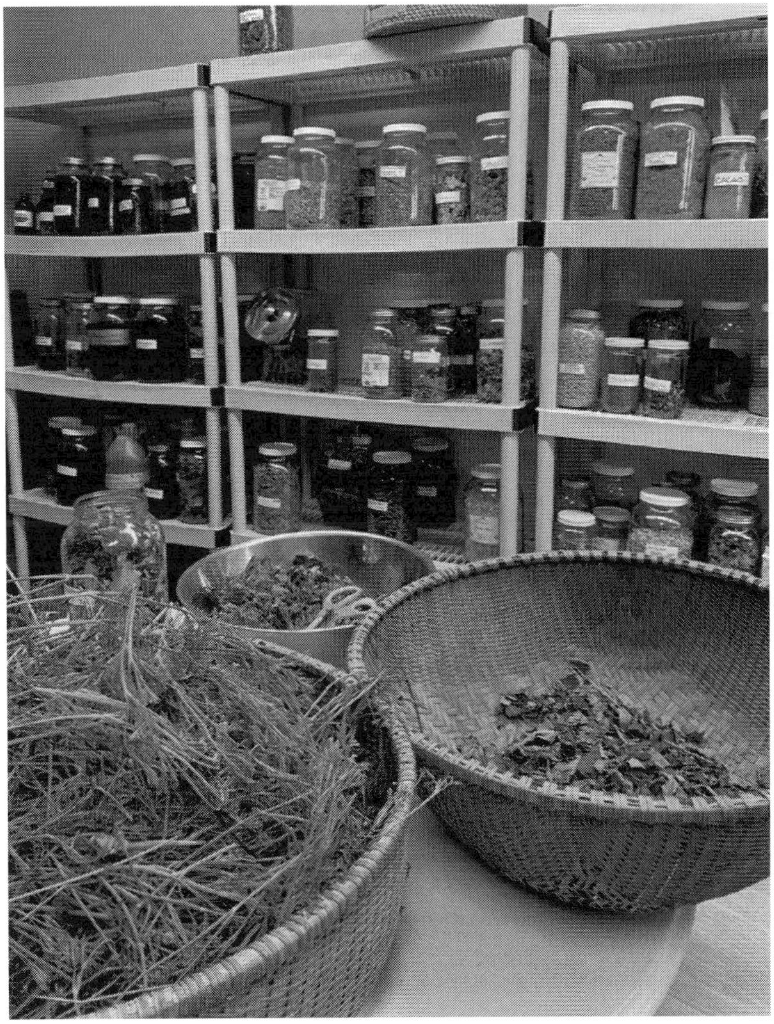

Please don't hate yourself, my friend.
You are the most jarring man
That I have encountered.

You rouse my spirit
The way in which
You steer my heart
And have stolen my bed.

There is none other like you
In this world, to me.

If you find
There truly is something
You do not accept in yourself
A way you are behaving
A pattern you keep repeating
A secret you are hiding
A lie you are selling. . .

I will be there, waiting.
A reward well earned
A person to tell you you're worth Something.

-a calling (to be better)

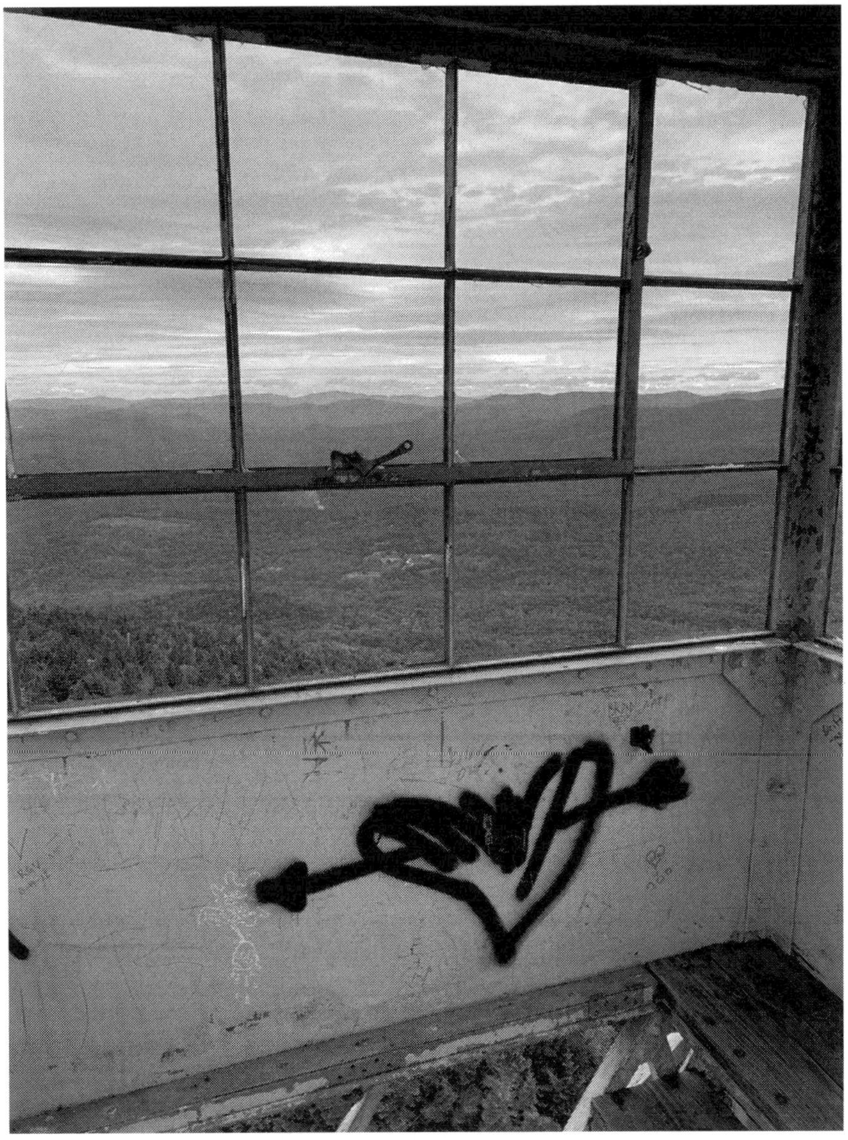

I can count on one hand
The men that have
Made me feel safe
In this world

And you are bright among them.

Compassionately, I accept you.
You're glowing, a soft blue light.

Come bring your earth-breaking, wood-splitting hands
(And their firm stroke)
To stay between my soft, plump thighs

Here can be their home
A place you will know
You are seen & appreciated.

-a soft woman's love

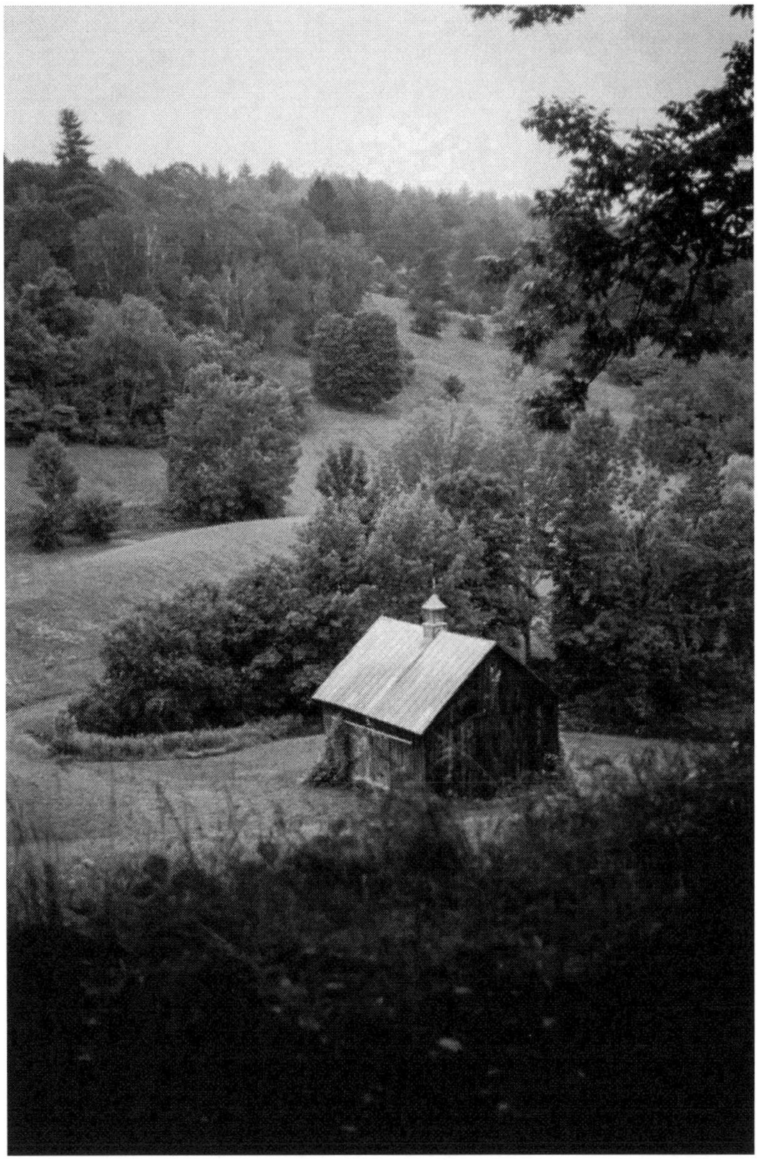

My sun-kissed lasso
Of flaming strawberry locks

Flutters in the wind

Gets tangled in your
Beard when we kiss

Little sparks in the air between us

-of air and fire

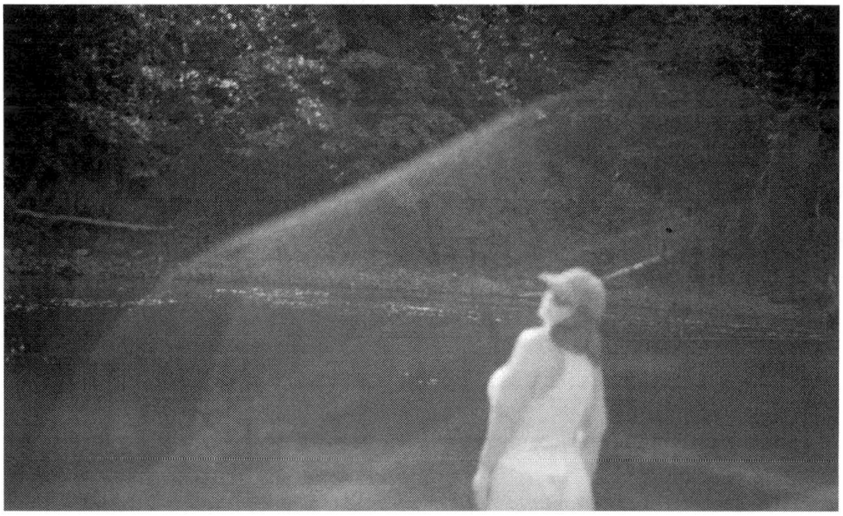

Always break for snapping turtles
And deer, and bear, and moose
Or any wild thing-

The respect and cohabitation of nature here is unmatched
Why can't the larger society live like this?
With autonomy of Self yet kindness for Others?
Allowing everything to have its place, without
Trampling over, conquering all?

So here, my generous heart will wait for the animals to pass
It gives me a chance to sing along to songs
Or focus better on my surrounding
Appreciate finding pleasure in a pause

-little worlds we ignore

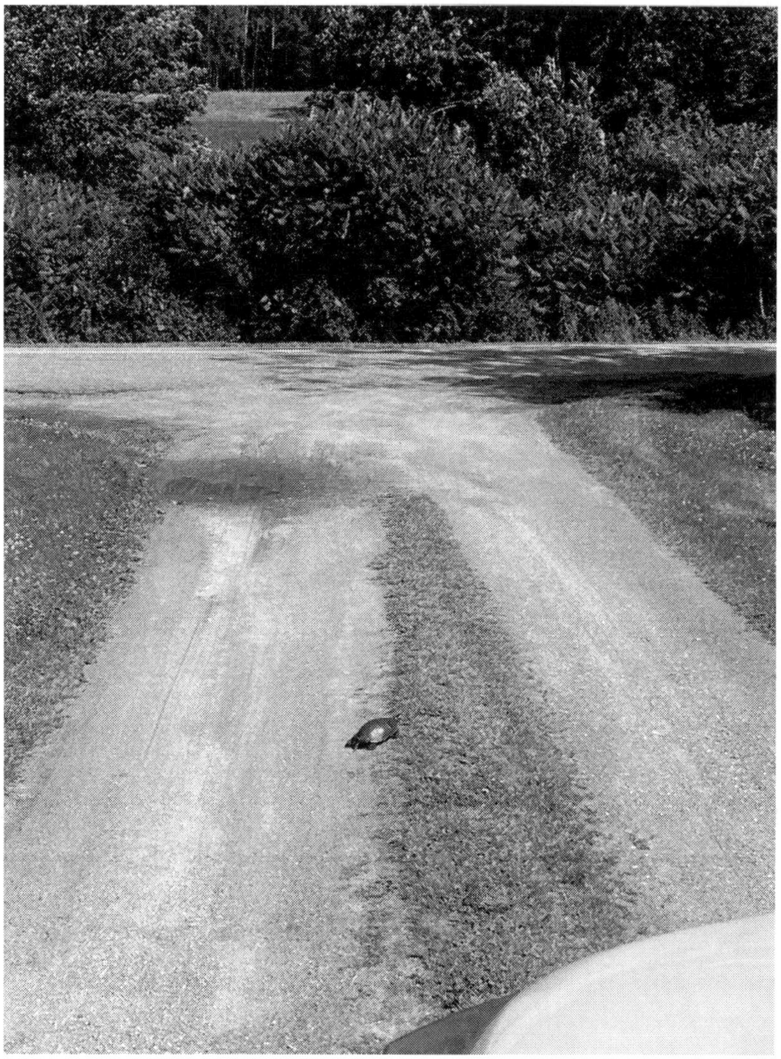

Here I am,
        Now!
(that is all there is in Life as the Past is dead and the Future unborn)

Connections like this are not so frequent.
We are natural magnetic energies.

Your heart reacts to me,
I can feel the comfortably ease
And the climaxing ecstasy
Rising in you when I'm nearby.
There is thunder between us.

I am your Sun:
        An earnest reprieve
From the inner turmoil

Lap me up from every opening
        & trust me when I say you are worthy.

-a tempting

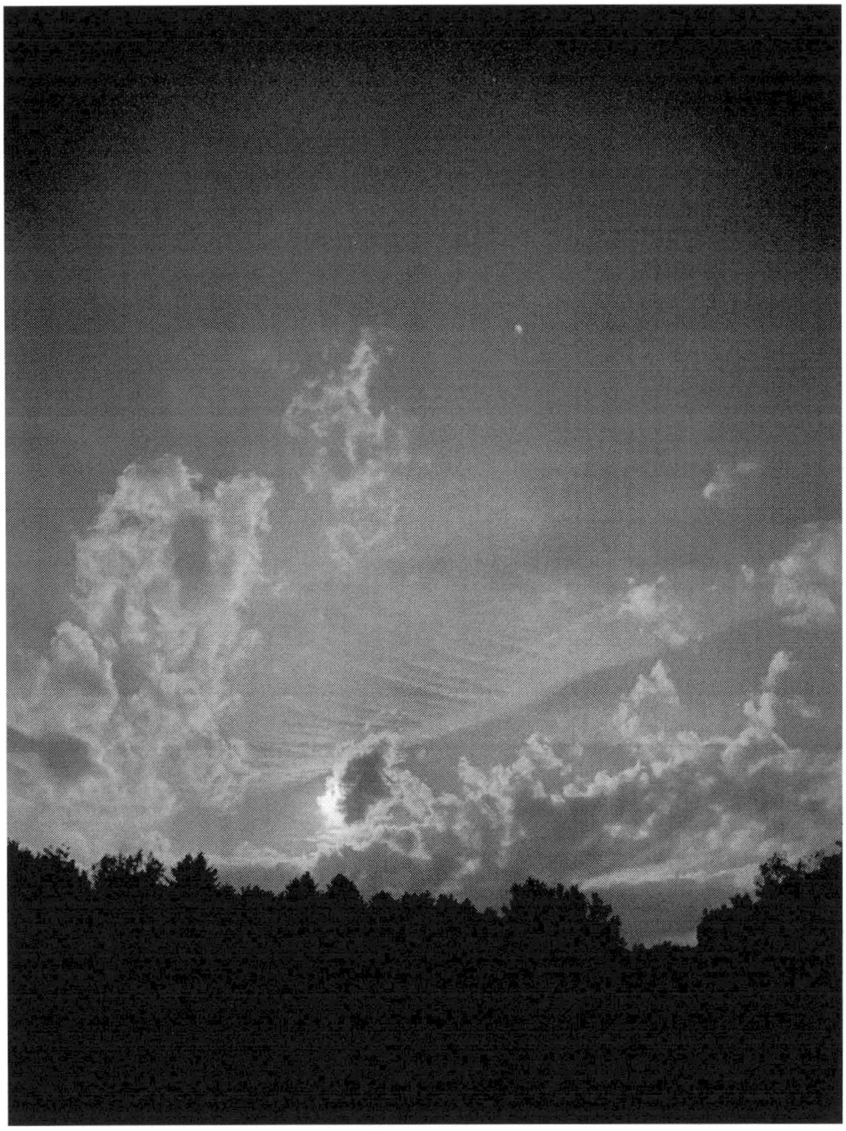

On the Kancamagus Highway
My heart unfastened wide
And took everything in.

Each tree and limb
Jumping fish and river bend
Waterfall and cloudy peak took me in.

I waded in a river stream
Admiring the rounded stones,
Each placed by God himself

Just so.

-this great unknown

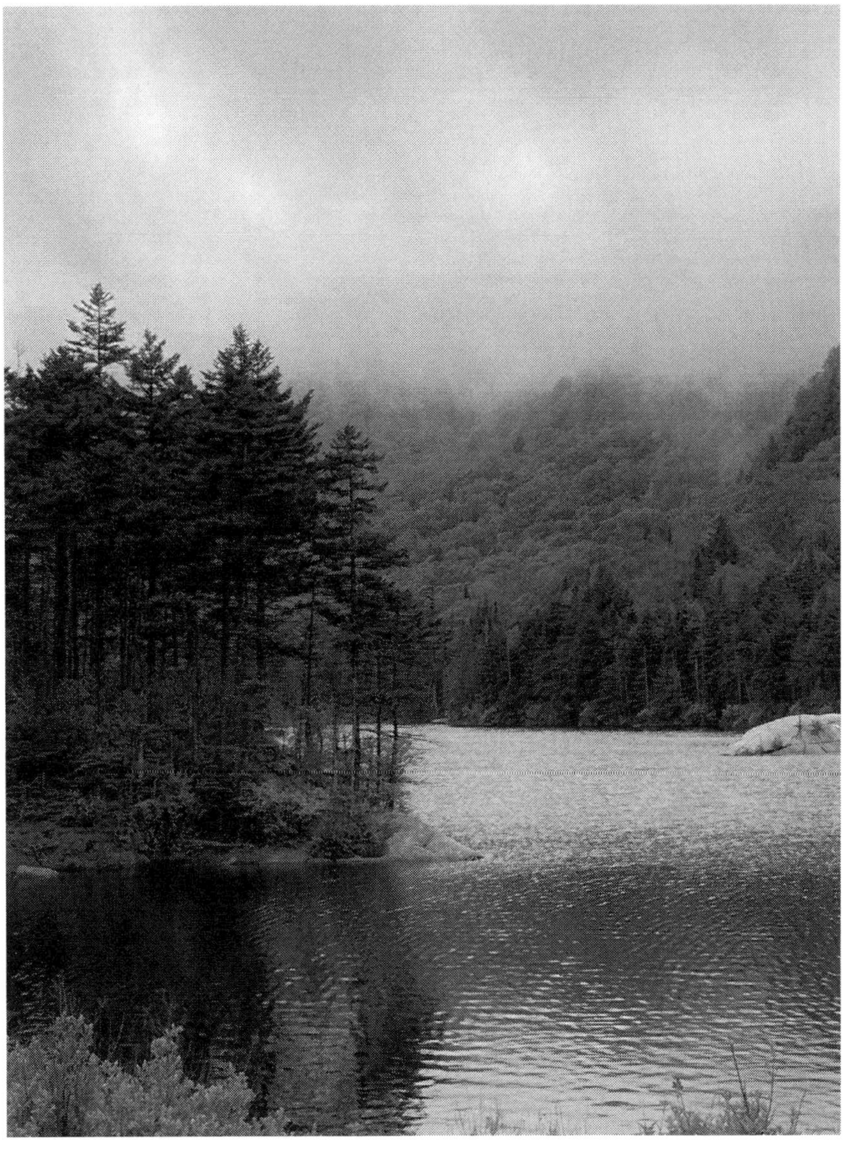

On a rainy summer afternoon
Here in the upper East Coast
Of New England

I make it a point
To jump in the pool

Bubbling at the surface
Sixty or below outside
Water droplets pounding on the wavy surface

It's important for the body
To feel new
Sensations
Uncommon vibrations
Heart pulsations

A sting to the breathwork
A jolt of adrenaline
A shock to the familiar

Live outside of routine.

-be a child again

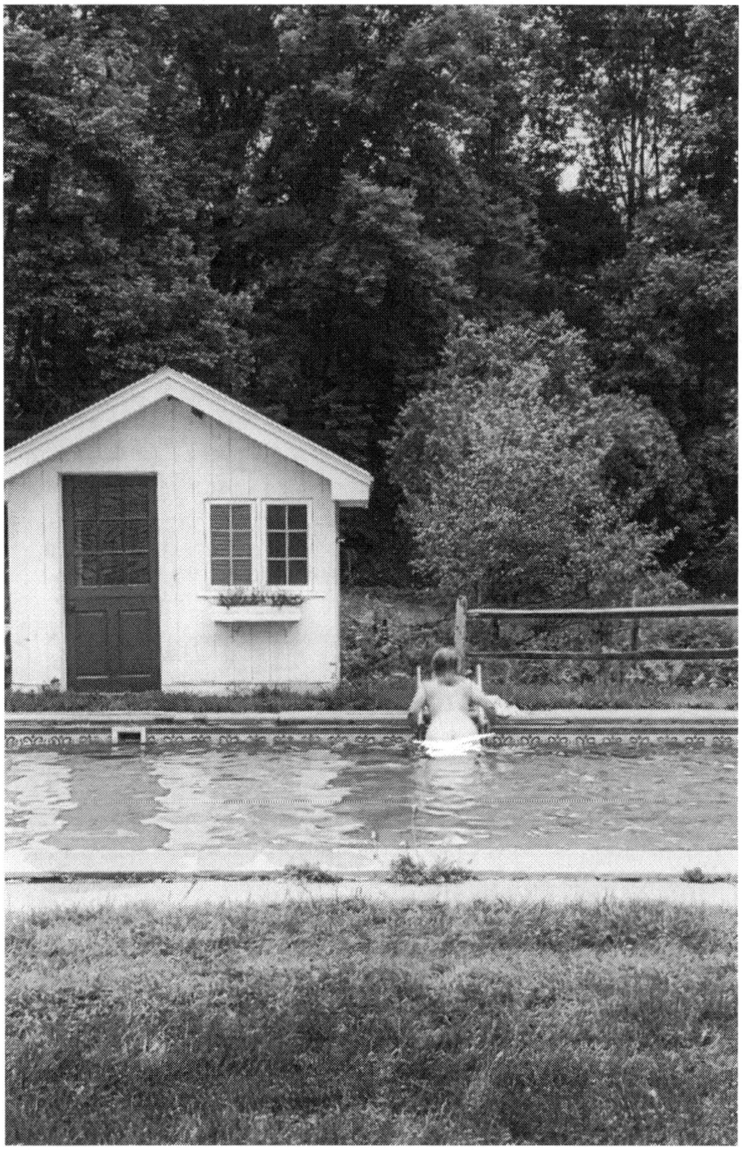

He reads me Kerouac
And the local paper
I sip on water
Or wine

       And admire.

We search for Moose
       along the Canadian border
We play chess
And laugh
       (we're still tied)

He shoots off bottle rockets for us at night
I watch excitedly in my blue and white striped shorts
His grey sweatshirt

We bring out a mattress to the top deck
Laid with sleeping bags & pillows

Entangling his hard body with my soft form
Shaking, squeezing, pulsating bliss
       All through the night

Everything here is fine
       Up at camp.

-things used to be alright

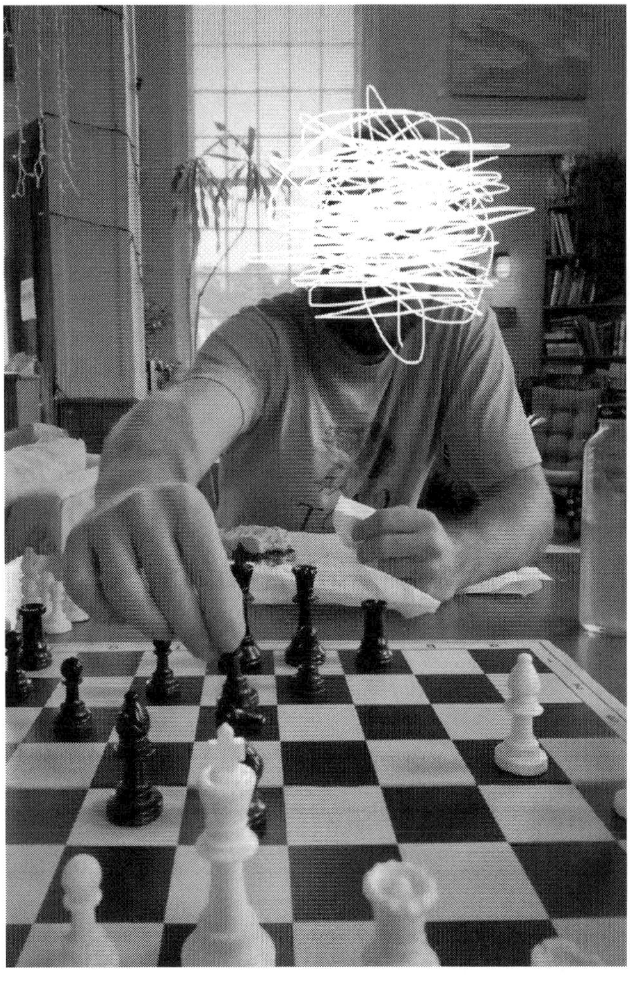

Sacred nectar spilling
From the crevice of my hidden place
Falls into your

      Smiling mouth

Your eyes widen
And then close indulgently

Sweeter than the maple syrup being made in the sugar house.

-crystalizing

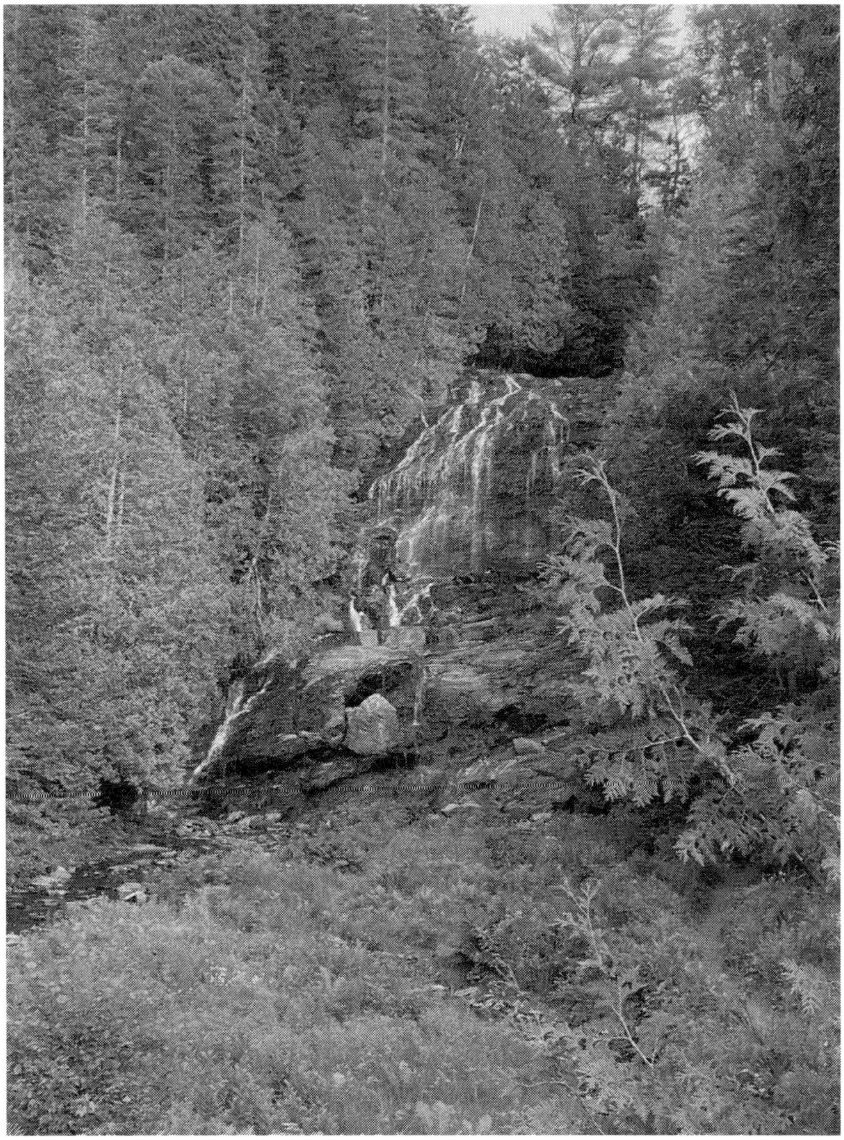

Your textured, rough, and tender hands
Cupped my body perfectly.
With supple care you gripped my hair
With intense and thoughtful control
Your tongue (delighted!)
Woven in all my buried places
You loved to smell me there
& never wanted to stop tasting me
Around the fireflies
Next to the river
Among the ferns
In the cabins
Under the shooting stars
On the sandy lagoon shore
That hidden roadside (where you pulled over)
Or the bed of your truck in the mountains,
At our spot.

So many times,
Dusted with stars, the night sky encouraged us along

Opening myself to you
Wider, broader, and deeper still
While you examined in blissful awe
Those green-blue eyes shining
Brow furrowed up with pleasure
& concentration

You always held me while we slept
Even if just my hand.

Forehead kisses
Sending me off to blissful slumber.

-insatiable

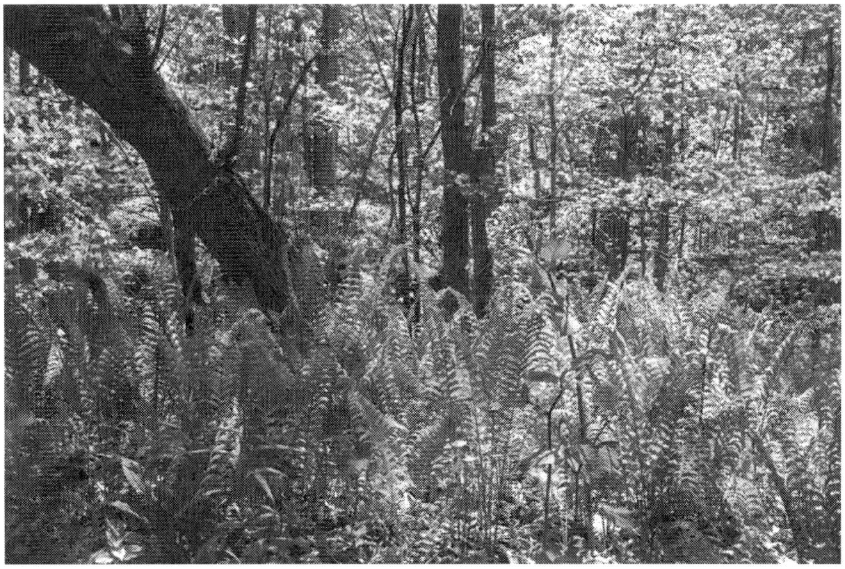

The day I saved myself
From dying on Mount Washington
A rainbow made me cry

It was stupendous, amazing!
Sandwiched between my near death
And dogged perseverance.

I couldn't shake the incident for days.

My takeaway is this:
Whether it ends slowly or quickly
For us all it is certain
To end.

I'll never waste one single
Unrestrained, adoring thought.
Never hide an ounce of my aspiration
Or grief
Compassion
Or fury

Because (for now) I am alive!
And I soak in the unbelievable
Pleasure-full agony of that timed certainty.

-conquering cliffsides

85

I was terrified to jump off the big rock
Afraid to scrape my leg
You big lug, you carried me –
Down and all the way to shore

Just a couple of kids playing
On an Indian Summer day
Camp Tamakwa calling our names

You grilled us fish in the heat
While I sang "more than a feeling" in jest
We got to know each other with vulnerability
And ate at your family picnic bench

These are the moments I'll relive
When you cross my mind

-a summer feast

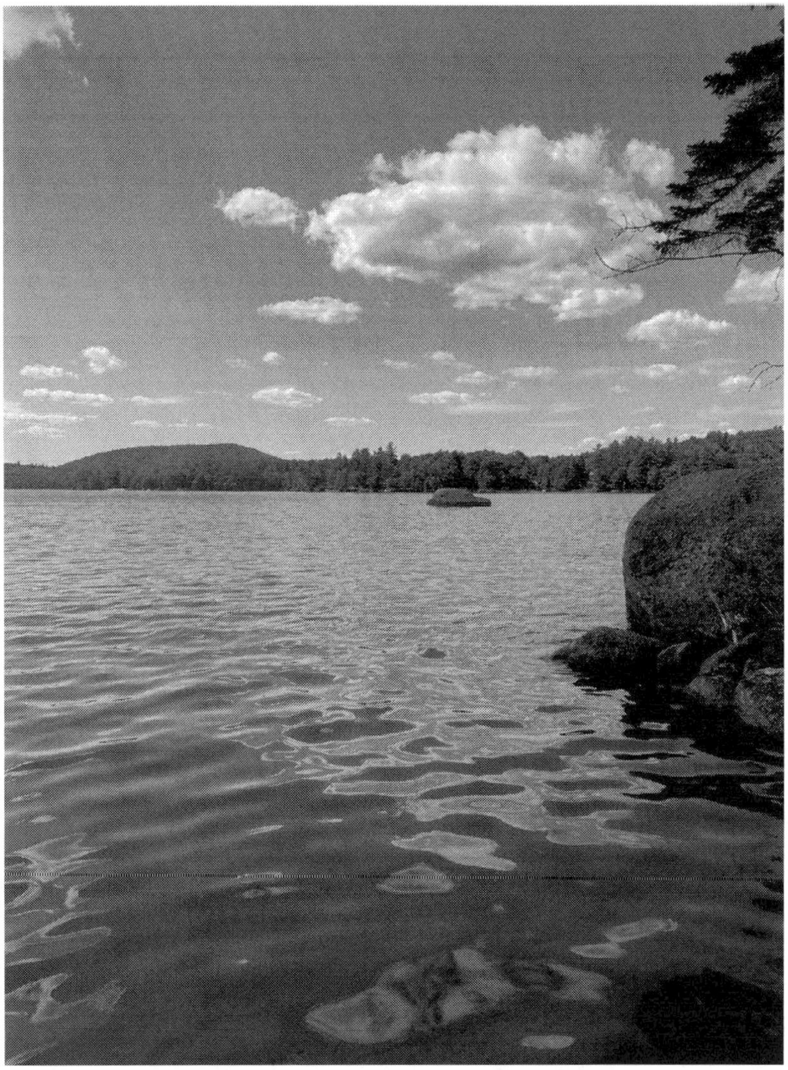

It took us a few hours to finally get up to camp
The family history was palpable, just in the air
A small forest of ferns surrounding the cabin
Twining around the birch trees

We were such a mercurial pairing,
I'm not sure what we were thinking
But it felt real good at the time

-a ride of sorts

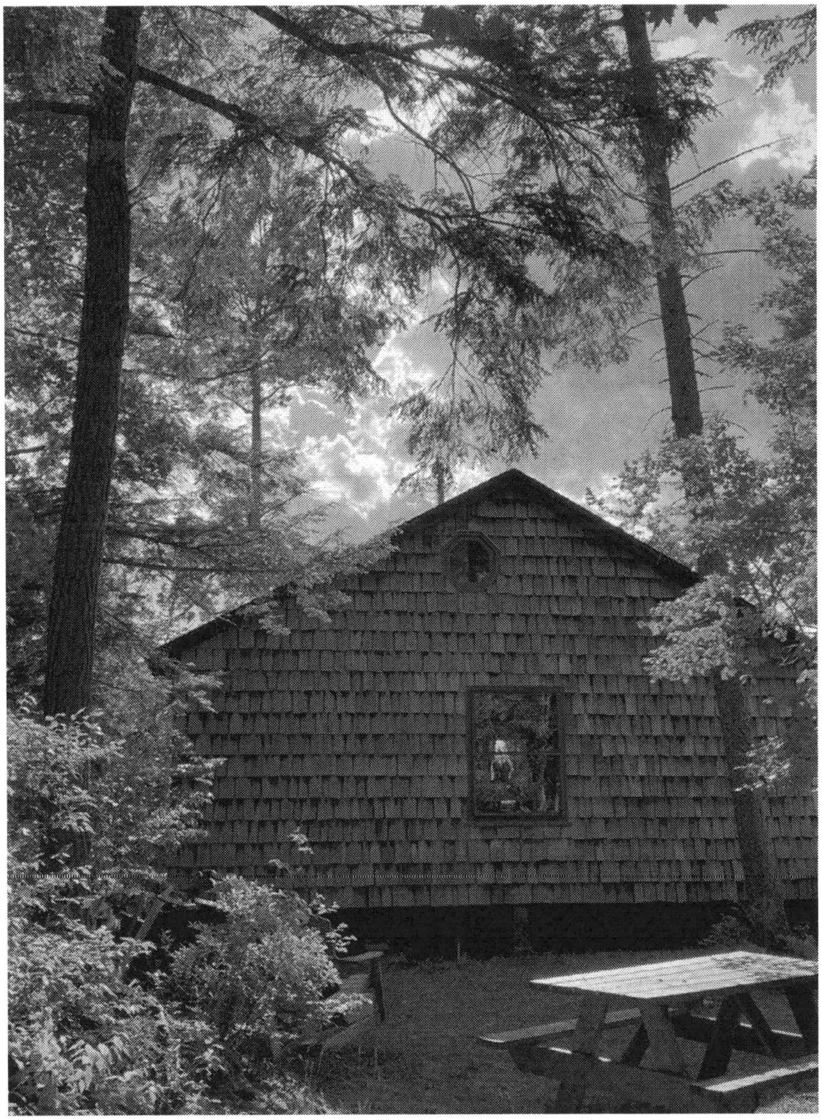

I love to hear your voice
Say my name

When you are out breath
Shaking

Near the peak
Of this mountain we've climbed

Lavishly watching you
Smile at me in these moments
When you are looking down at me

Then your knees
Are tired but
Keeping us interlocked, you begin again
Cradling me to the side
We continue to rock into the night.

-*animals*

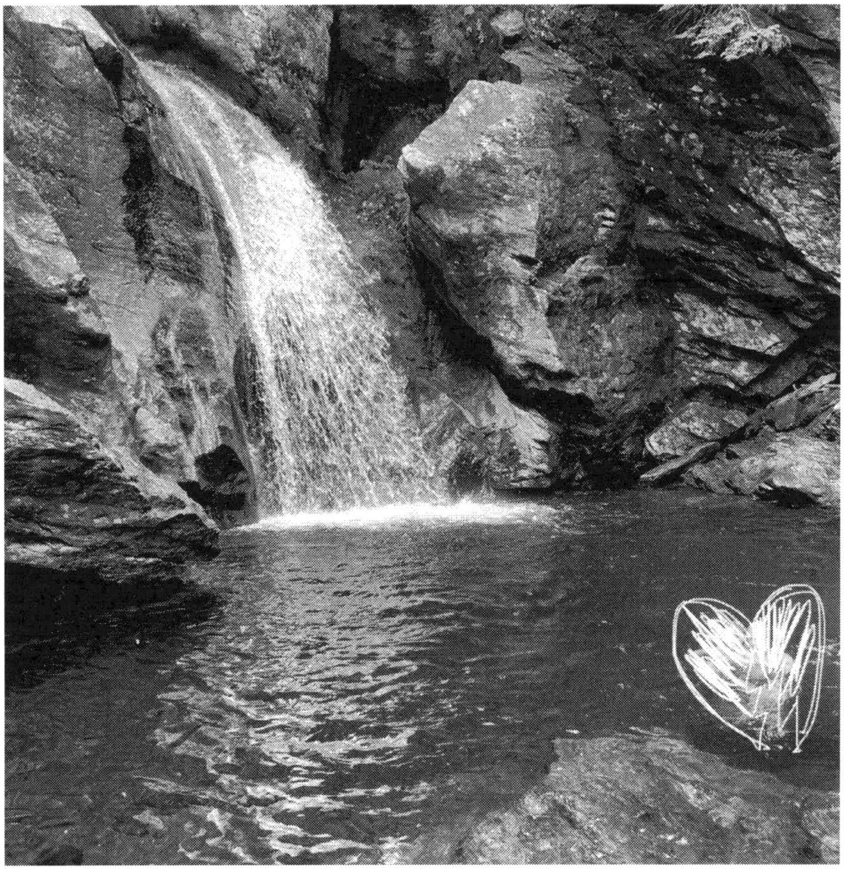

I pulled his head
Onto my lap
Hoping he could feel
Some inner peace
Flowing through our united energy
& just how captivating
This dynamic is between us.
I gave my body & heart so freely.

He went home & made plans with other women.

-a divide begins

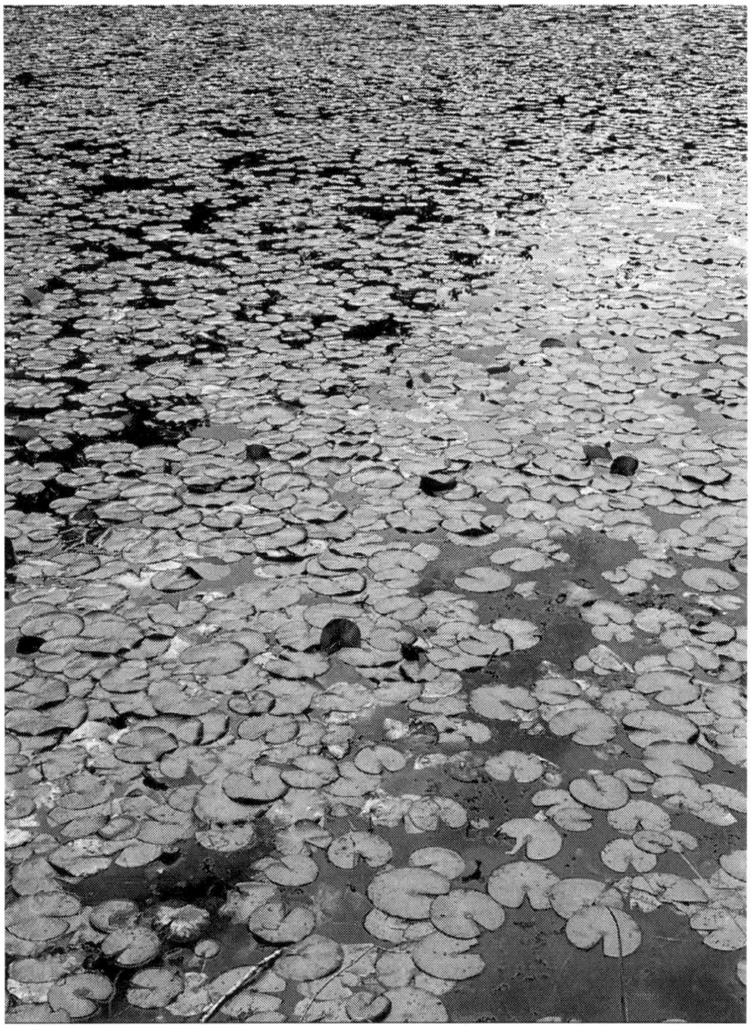

Spent the day mining
The milky quartz veins
Over in Maine
Finding garnet and tourmaline
Hiking back sweaty but gleaming like
The treasure in my pack

A brisk dip in the icy sea afterwards
No one in the water but me
Atlantic body blessing mine

Racing the clouds to
Reach the edge of the storm
Just the sky and me
On an old two lane
Heading back to the Green Mountains

-mine Maine

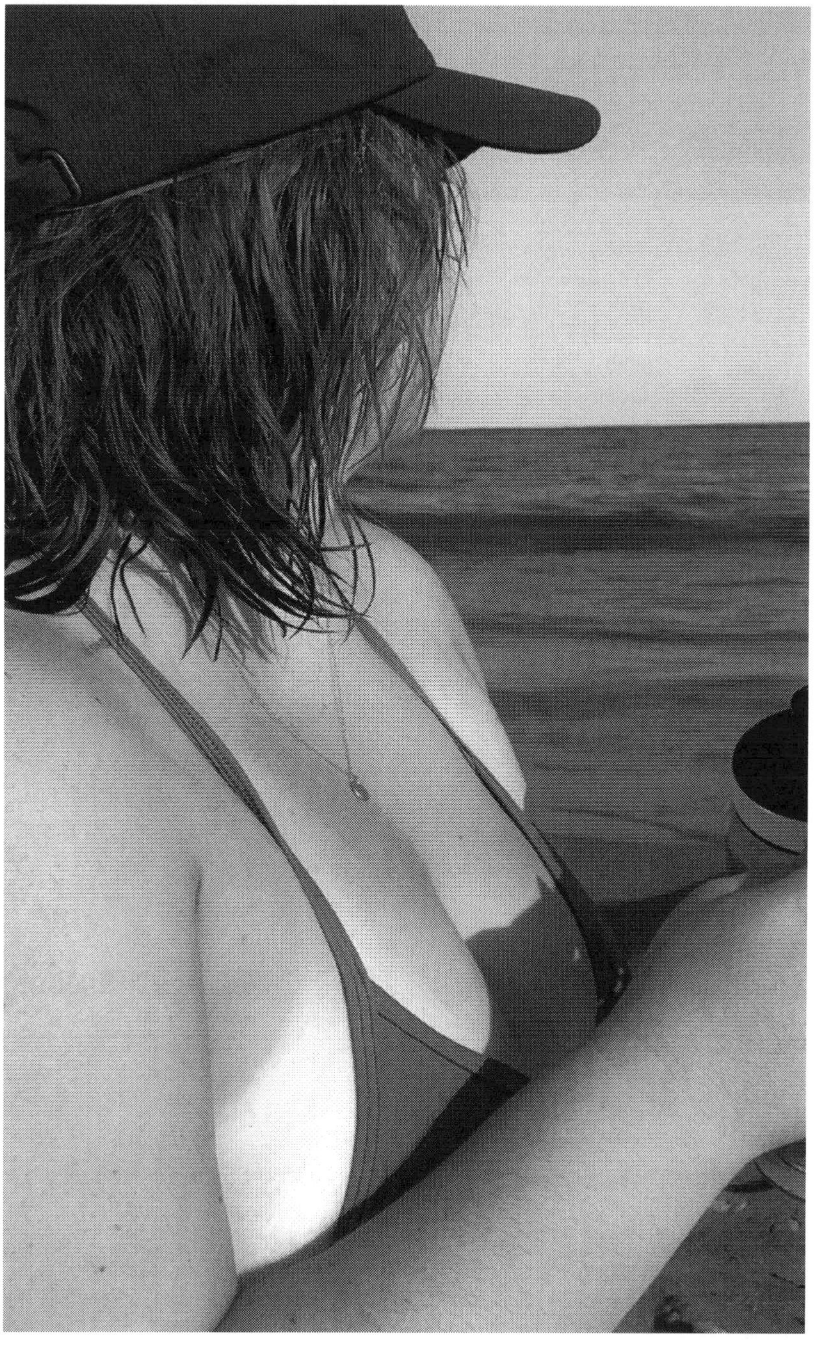

I will be the brave one
Ever-loving with all my might

Forever watering
Your cool, dark places.

I rather love others to
The best of my ability
In this life
On my level
In my way
By my means

Unswayed by their incapability.

-a woman who dares

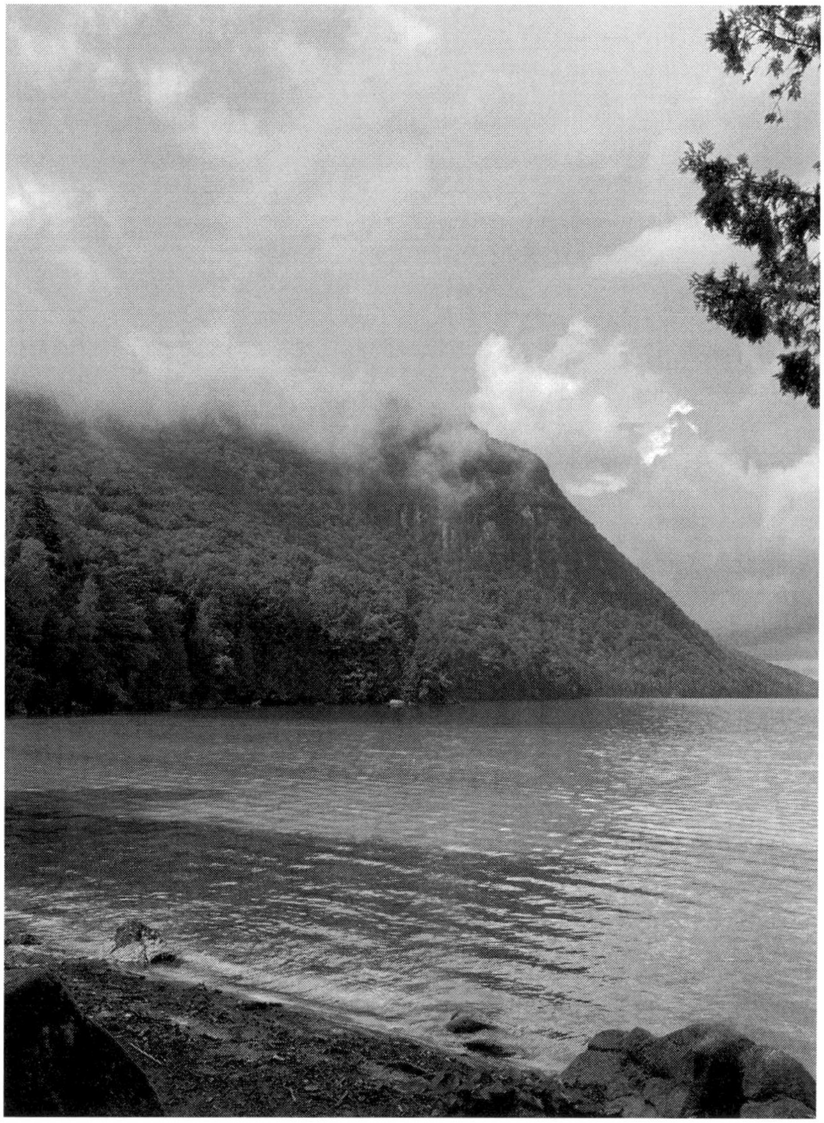

At the foot of the mountain I am no one
Insignificant and small
Humble servant to the winds
The terrain

At the top of the mountain I could be anyone
A star or scientist
Or survivor of many trials
Even a triumphant rejoice of life
A diamond amongst the pebbles

The mountain grinds me down
And what remains may appear brittle
But is the strongest sinew of my life
I carry these scars with pride

-*measuring up*

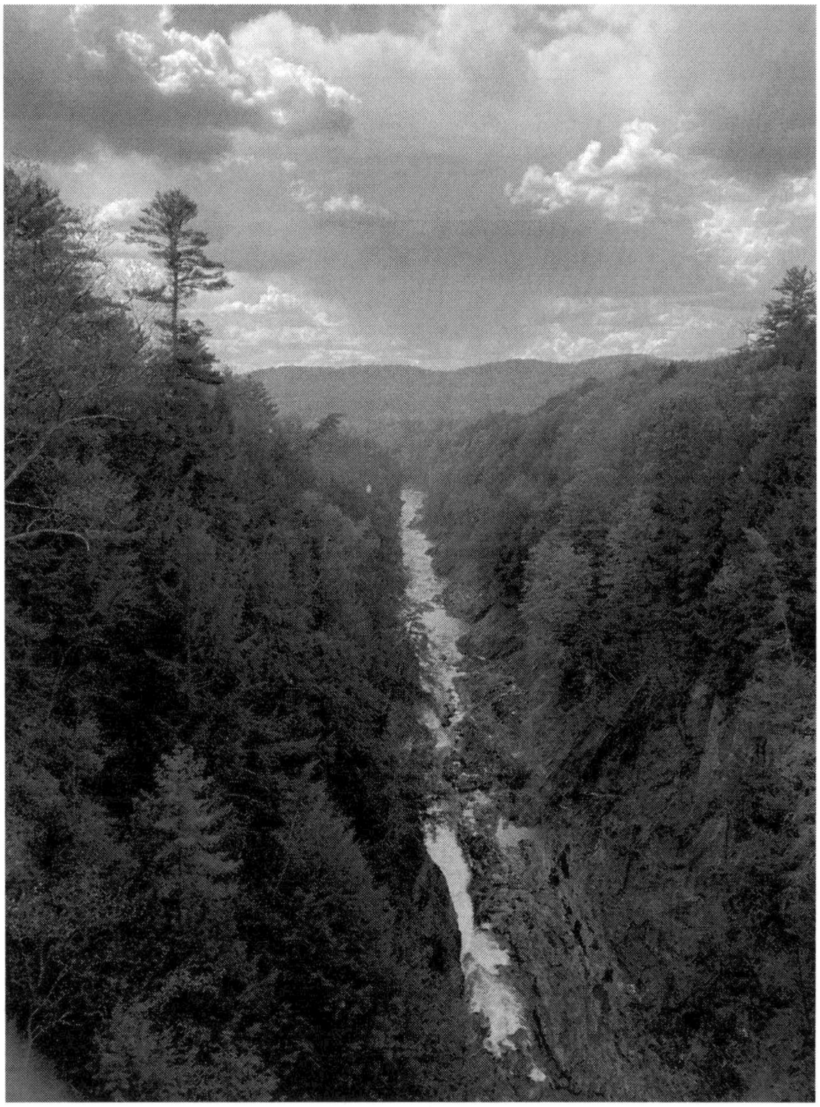

My new guy is a high jumping
Free flier
A deep breathing ocean diver
And he's held his breath for me
The captain of this yacht and my heart
We spend the weekend camping among bears
Along the river, fly fishing and star gazing
He serves me smoked muscles by the fire
And tells me tales of Drakensberg,
Of his Andalusian horses
And the last time he lost his heart

A strong cortado in the morning
At the nearby chalet I practice my Afrikaans
Sweet kiss goodbye and see you next time
I'm near the coast of Maine

-*Oh, Captain Nick*

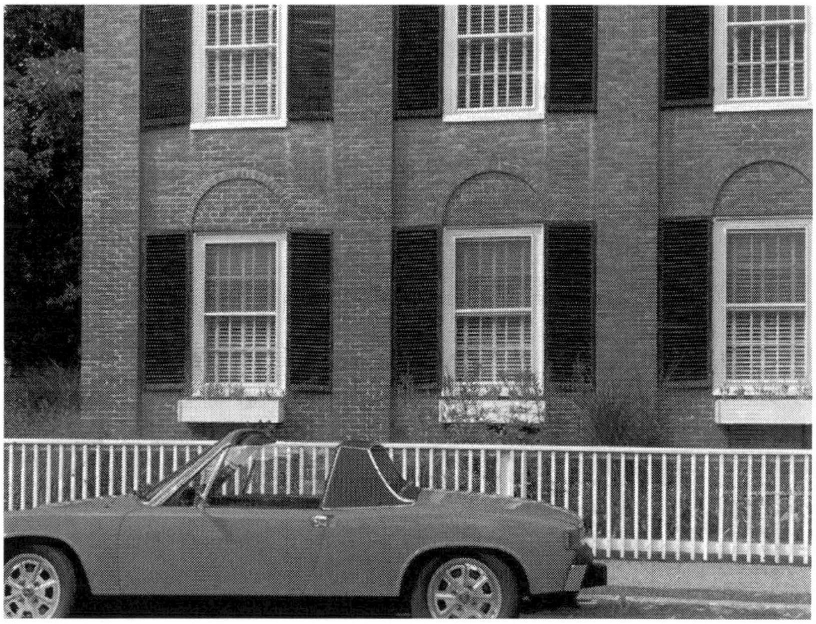

Lake Champlain guide me
Your gusty shores hit me hard
The epicenter of the chaos

I wanted to love you but
You just wouldn't let me
Your roaring winds
A perfect soliloquy of my time there

-too big to put my arms around

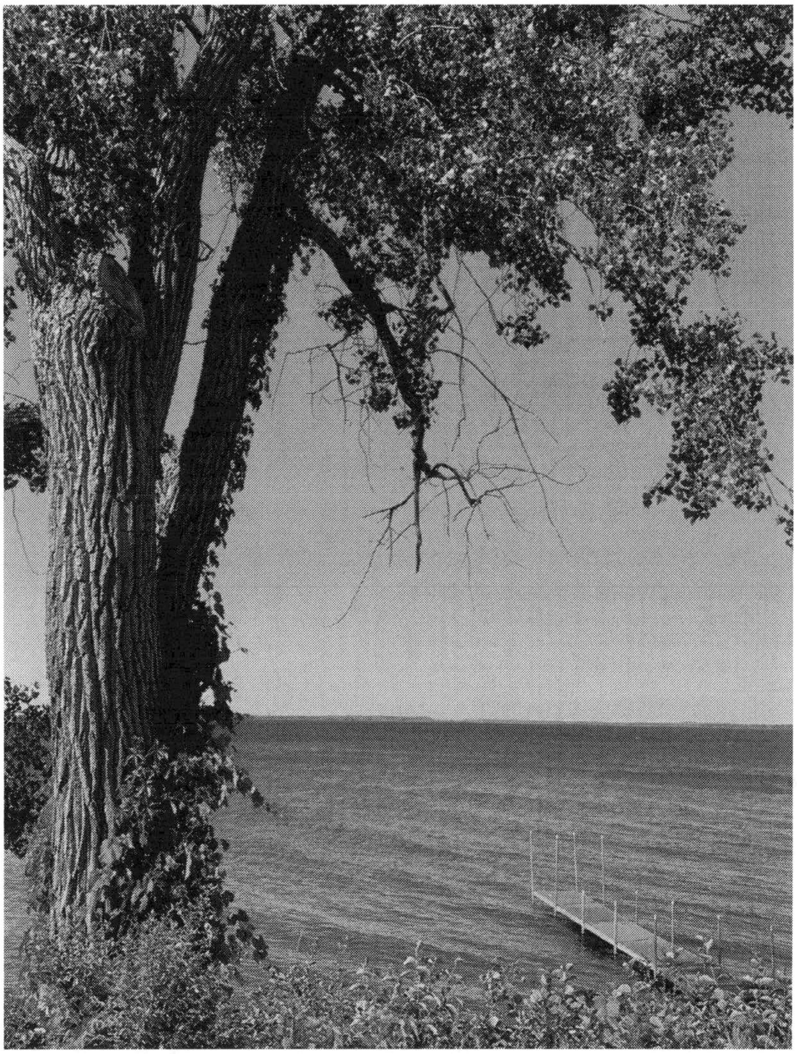

The last storm that came through
I was so afraid

In California I've never seen such close lightening

I took the path through
The thick woods to your cabin
You were smiling, shirtless and warm
Laughing at me
Through the window frame
Over your kitchen sink

I ran inside
Soaking in my cardigan
Feeling relief and safety
From your presence.

I love the smell of you
And of the wood
      In the shed you built.
      In the stacks surrounding your yard- kindling for winter.
      In the walls of logs outlining your home.
      In all the covered bridges in the place you grew up.

How I wish we could recall scents like memory.

-views from a cabin

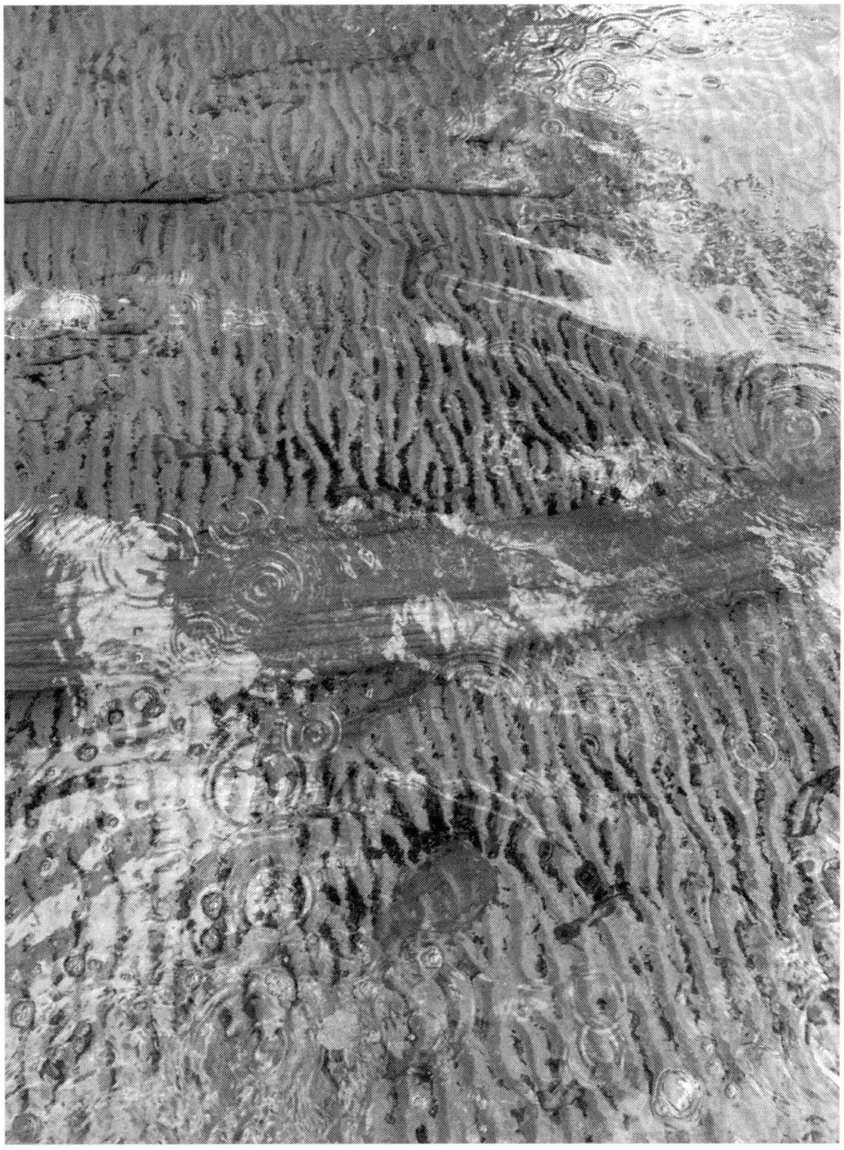

She only calls me
Mermaid

Or Mighty!

We sit by the pond
And conspire.

We wait for Jodie
& Ginger
By the bonfire.

We drive around
Listening to African music
And speak eloquently
Or have a sit in companionable silence
During the witching hour.

Her speeches and stories are lessons
On how to live a rich life in love-
Of dancing with yourself,
And of loving or losing partners.
A lecture on regrets.

-*amicable wisdom*

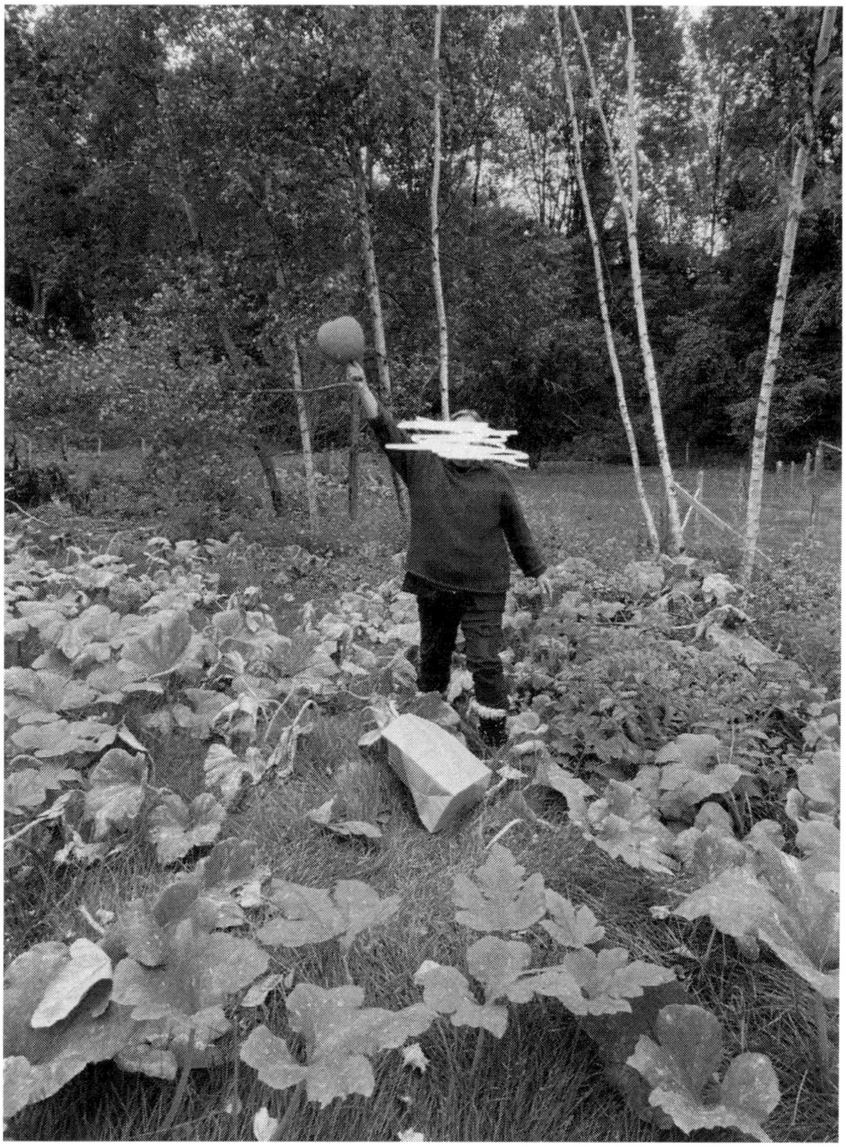

Bearded big-bellied man
Meditating his mantra at the lake
Told me it was a vortex, that mountain place.
I've half a mind to believe him
Because I keep coming back
For the peace.

Topless, I cleanse my soul in the chilly waters
While admiring the background chatter
Of the Quebecois visitors.
Hours pass.
A dragonfly kept landing
On my straw hat all afternoon-
Whisper to me the secrets you carry-
My spirit wants to fly with you, too!

-my favorite place

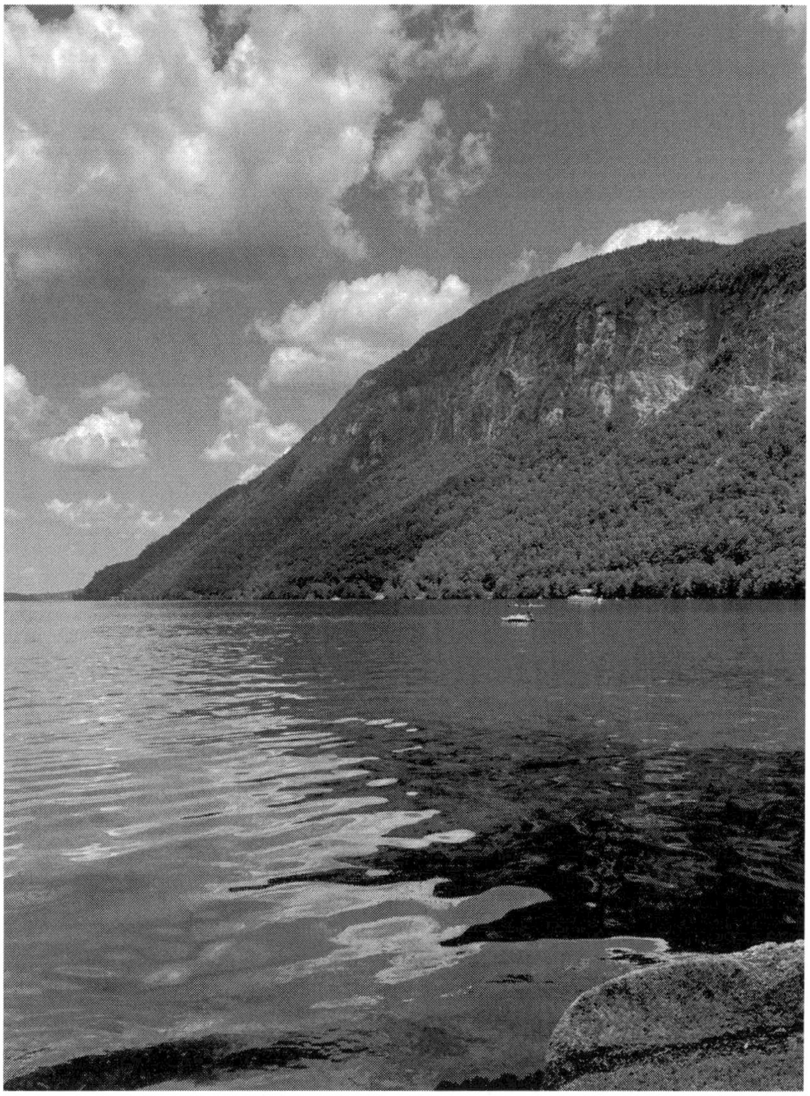

Goodbye sailor, off to Nassau
Waving off the rocky coast of Maine
It was such a lovely time
He didn't notice that he was leaving
Remnants of his heart in my hand.

-*a summer fling*

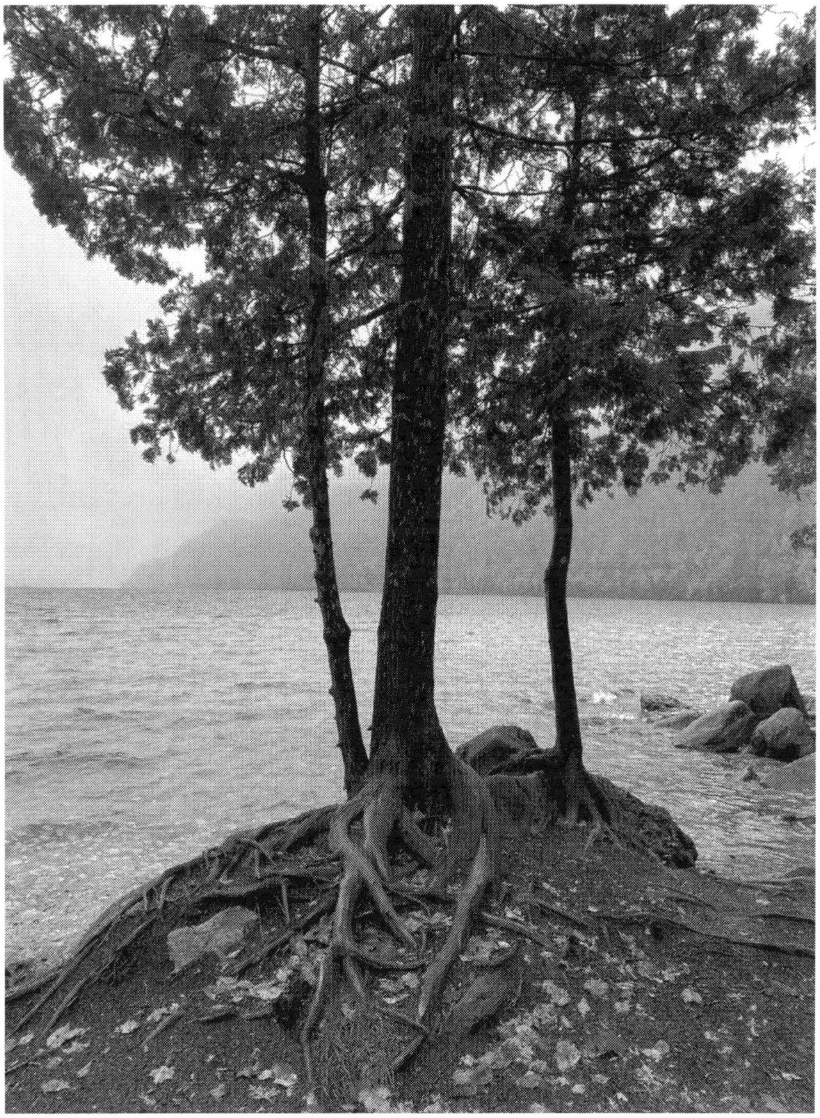

Dear professor from the lake today
Thank you for the sweet kiss.

Just two strangers of a chance encounter
Spending the day together
Wading in waters
Snacking on shore
You gently held my hand
You made my confidence soar
Souls connecting for an afternoon.
It was perfect like a short film
A five-minute memory of a life well lived

-but I can't recall your name

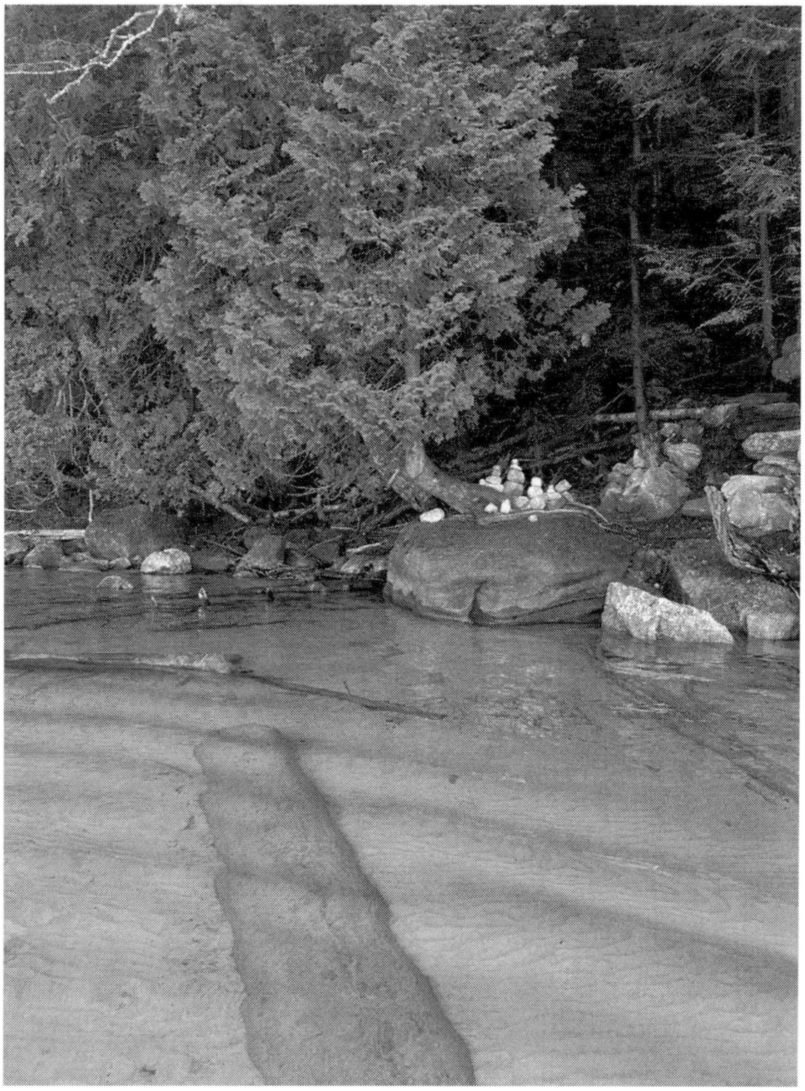

Wearing my navy tennis skirt & khaki body suit
You took me out on an early August night
We swam naked
In the glacial waters
Of the bowl-shaped lagoon
At our favorite spot

We made our shadows dance
On the opposite cliffside
(before & after we dipped in)

We ran barefoot between root and fern
Along the paved road
To sit warming naked
In the furnace of your truck

God, we were so sympatico last night
Calling each other "perfect"
In between kisses
And what felt like
Hundreds of thrusts

You sent waves of
Chills over my body
Volcanic & erupting so much
That I can recall them back
With ease today

Your touch has marked me. I'm yours.

-a night together

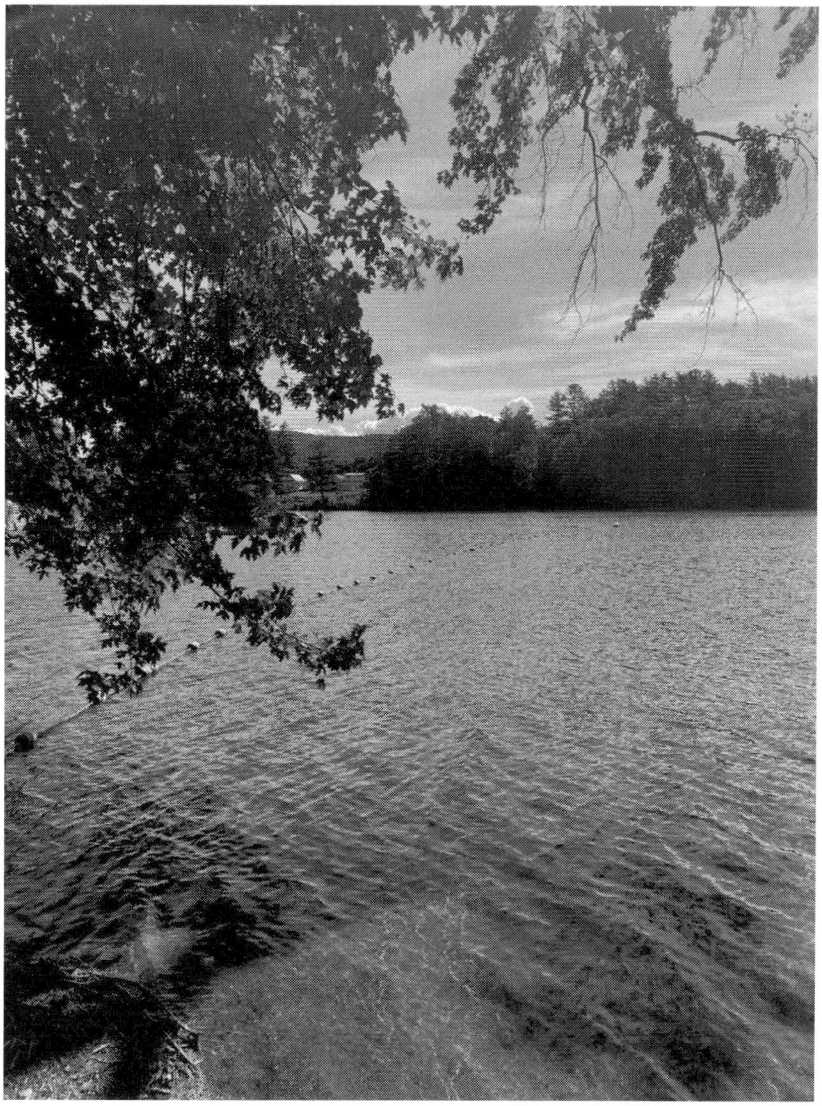

The stars came out tonight
While we were at the
Old drive-in theater.

A charming place
In the valley, between big, green hills
With an old school bus
For the concession stand.

Everything with you
Was out of a movie,
To me.

-beetlejuice at Bethel

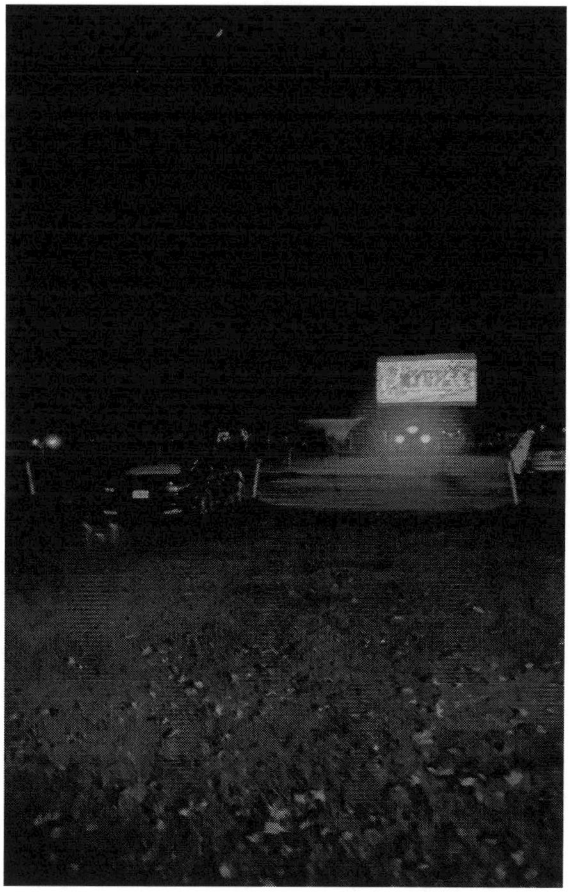

In my lengthy
Immaculate solitude
I ventured through
The shadow parts
Of my mind & heart

I wanted to clean
Everything out
So that I could
Make new again

      After healing.

To not live a life of
Old, broken patterns
Plagued by
Generational trauma
And splintered relationships
Fractured beliefs of
False rose-colored memories
Mud-stuck listening to
My inner critic's cruel voice

No, no this wouldn't be me

-breaking curses

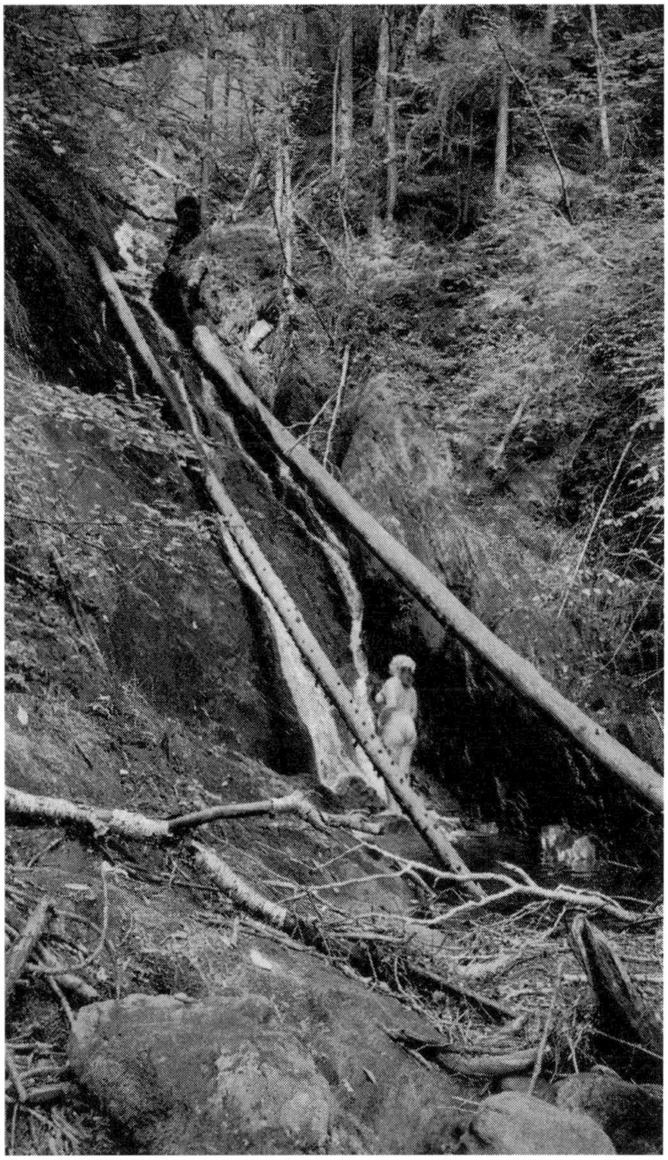

Short-lived seduction
From a man who lived in a shadowy cabin
On a hill in the woods
Born unto his small town.

I had envisioned hot fires on snowy nights
Building a home in the Northeast Kingdom
Watching bears from the porch
Cooking him meals
While the Stones were on the record player
Nourishing all his appetites
Each & every day.

But I was too much-
My valley girl voice
My animated energy
My grateful, and gracious heart
My expressive love of All.

He went back to his ashen life-
The familiar routine.
Crying, I ran away to find solace in the nourishing sun
Far away along the West Coast.

-*bad man bad timing*

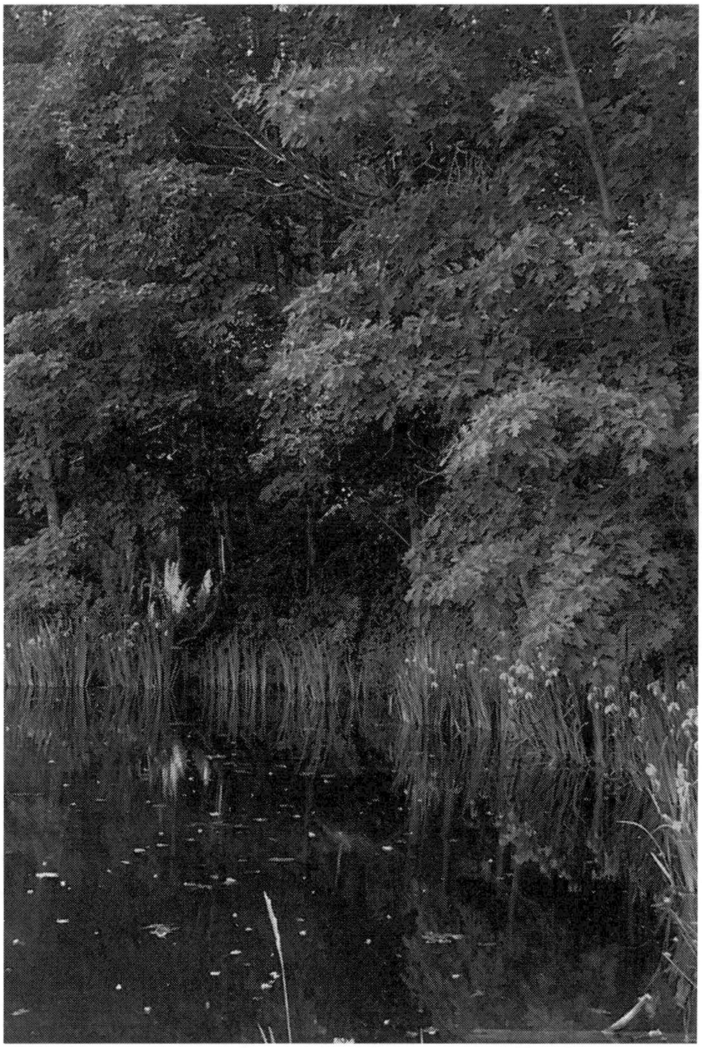

If I'm not getting
Out of this world
Alive
I will make messy, uninhibited love to my life
I will be damn sure to break my back
And bloody my palms
Living my truth
Shamelessly

Some say violently
With chaos
Delight
Whimpering
Crying in despair
Sometimes ecstatic
Elated
Rejoicing
Quivering
With delight

Indebted for this time.

-an unstoppable force

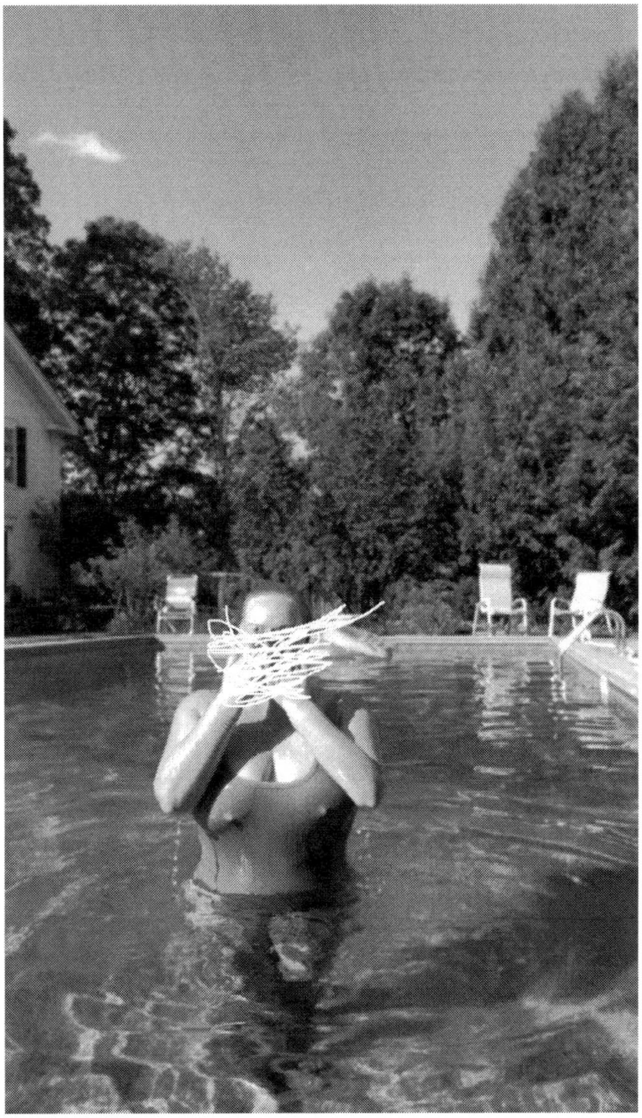

The blue heron
That moved into the pond
On the farm, watches me.

He's waiting for me to heal, I think.
Or reminding me of beauty in this Universe.

Sometimes he comes all the way to my window
At the farmhouse
And stands for so long,
Ever still from my view.

Other times he comes up
To the smokey wood on fire
And stays with me for hours.

As if nature is pleading with me
For some action I am still unsure of.

-signs from the world around us

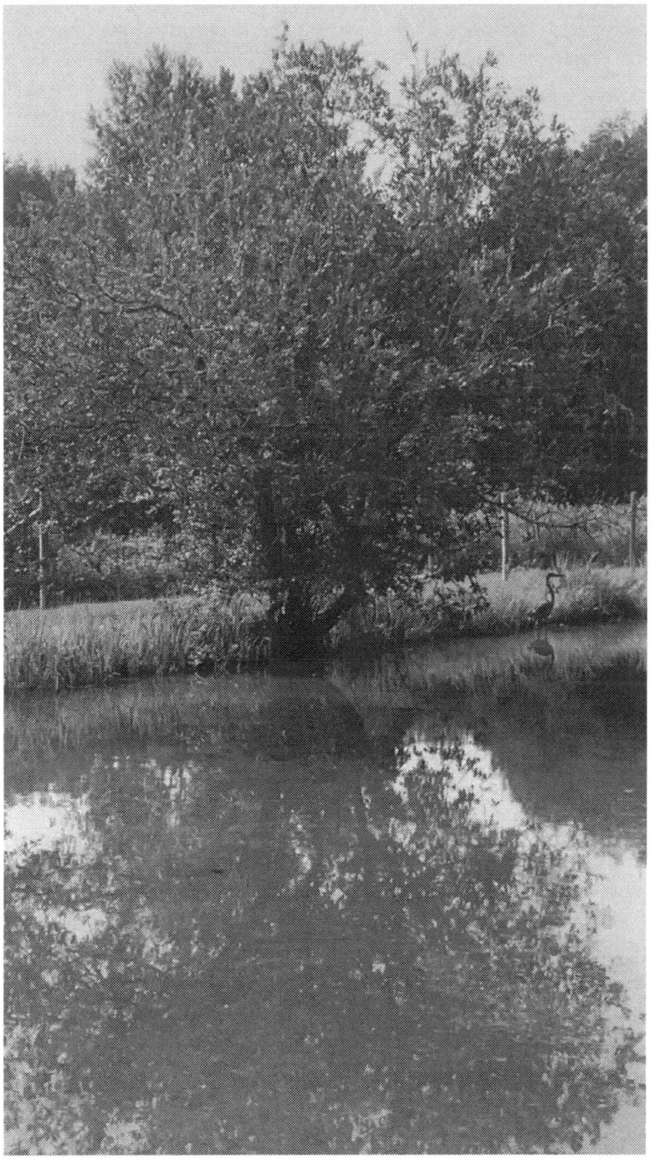

My summer in
The Green Mountains
Made me feel like I was seventeen again
Like life was laid out on the road ahead.

As I drove on alone on the ever long highway
Endless opportunities began to spread out
All before me, in my thirties.

Life never stops until you do.
Our lives are what we make of them.

I hadn't felt more attractive, powerful,
Craved or capable than in these days.

-a risk returning

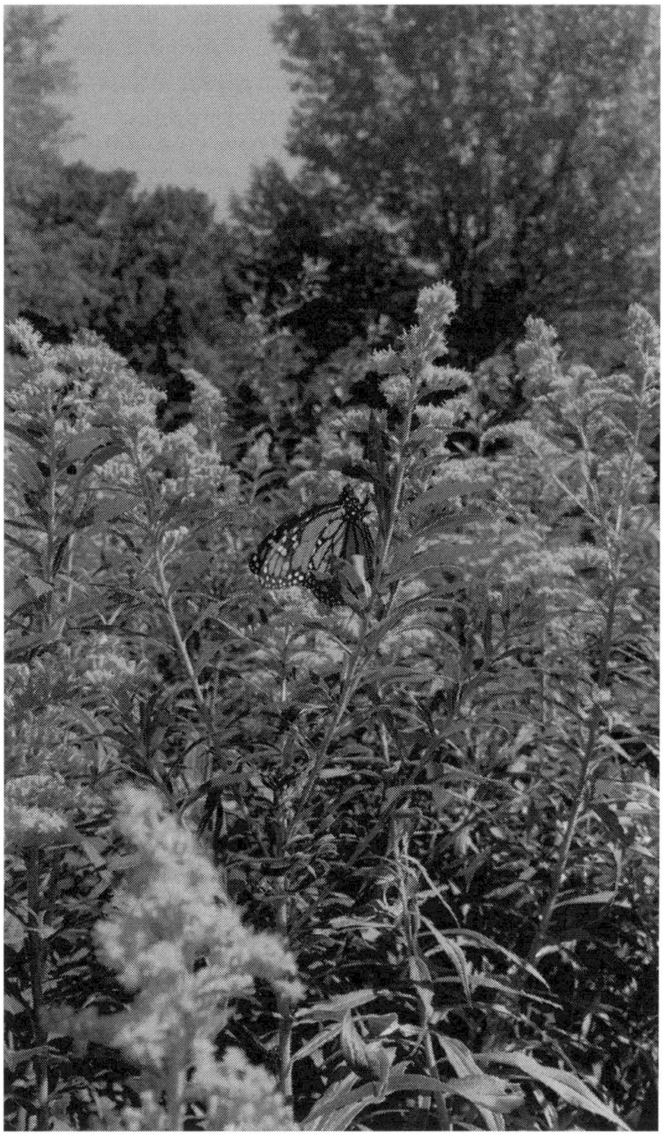

I'm so green

        Not new, green
But healing
        Lush!
        Alive!

Full of the wet soil
And rich air
Dancing around my curves
        And long tendrils

Amber fire light in my eyes
A fruitful woman
Barefoot
And naked in the river mouth

You hear the drum of my heart &
        It excites you every time.

-we are in constant renewal

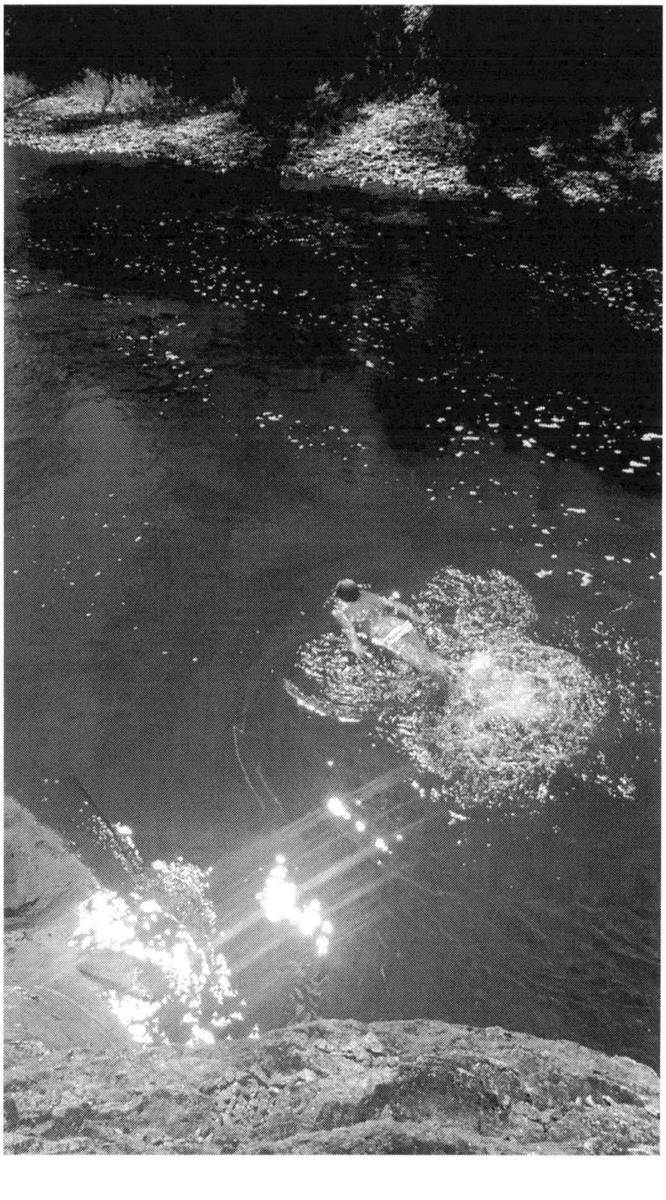

A summer renaissance
Learned self-assurance
Creative explosion welcomed me
My feet on the Earth
Grounded my soaring spirit
So that I was able to fly further and higher
Than I ever knew was capable

-a revival

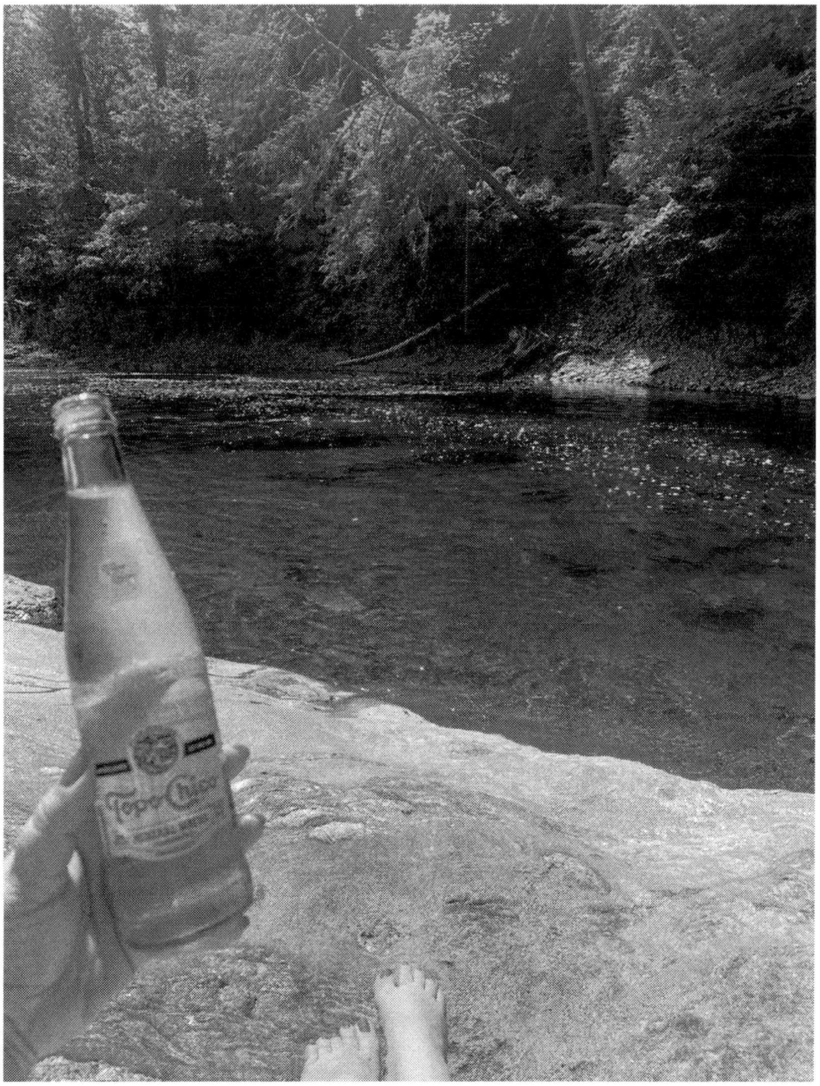
Topo Chico

All of life showed up for me

In New England

Thrill
Solitude
Friendship
Lust
Great wonders
Heartbreak
& perseverance

In compacted time I was brutally beat down
Punched by confusion
Experienced calamity
In cadence with the bullfrogs' tune

Yet there were so many
Reasons to rejoice

Running through the fields of tall grass
My battered breath in rhythm with the crickets

My spirit soared into the vast sky
And I found a good life

-a spectrum

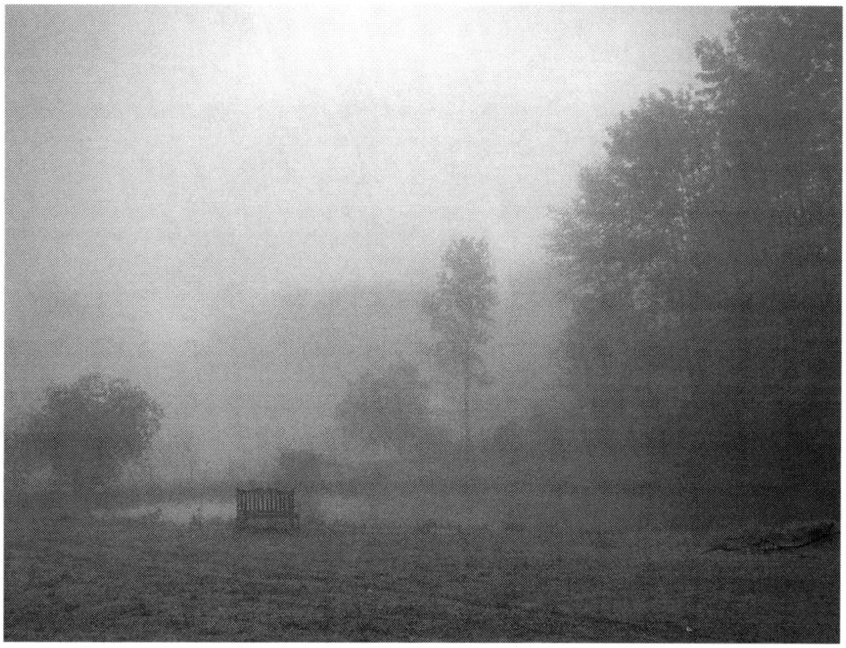

A storm killed
Our power tonight.

I sat out on the porch
With a candle
And my notebook.

I felt connected to the lightning
For the first time in my life.
In that same wondrous way
I usually feel out in nature.

We had a lengthy conversation
About power, fear, & the Divine.

Until the thunder bellowed
And I came to rest inside.

-a woman (un)afraid

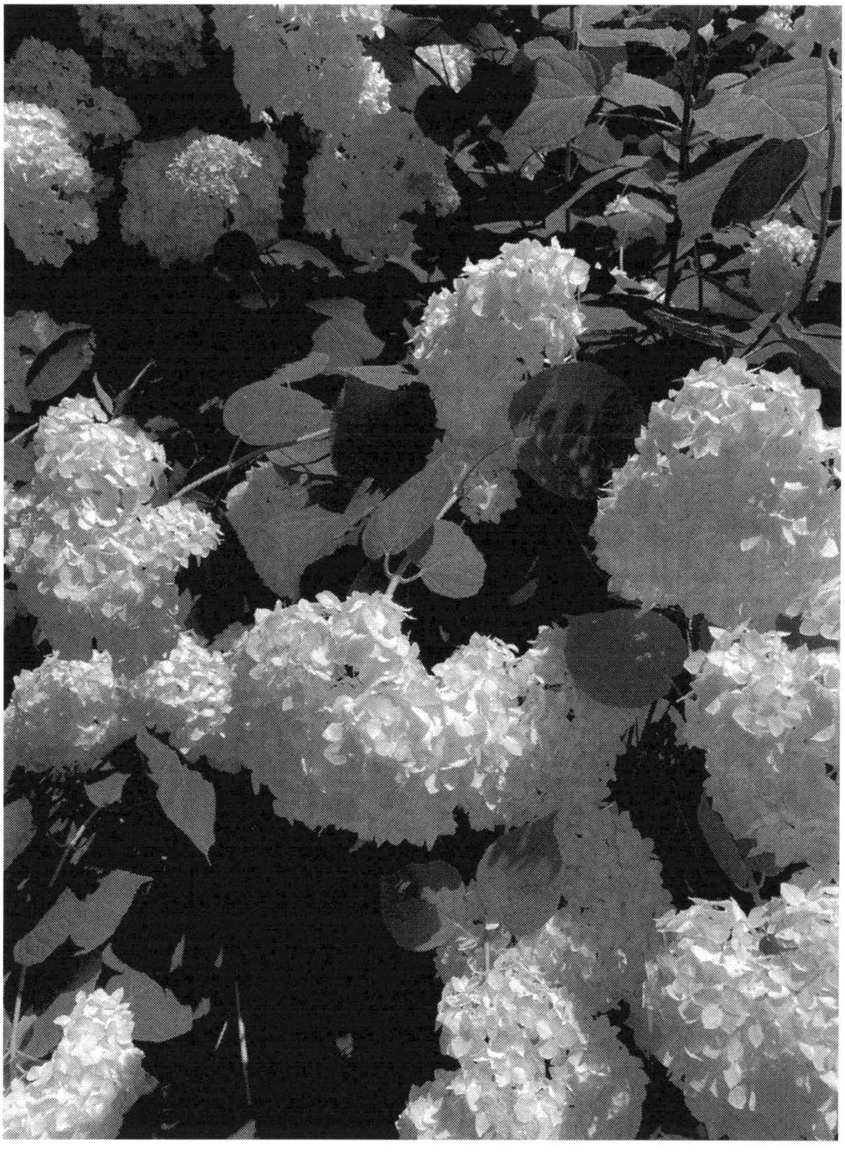

This summer in New England
Was flooded with
Record-breaking rains
Hurricanes.

A reprieve from the heat
And wildfires
That had already assaulted California.

This beautiful green place was awash in grey gloom.

Kind people,
Hard workers with rigid routines
Followers of their traditions
Reliving the same lives
Each season with great appreciation.

-*a living land*

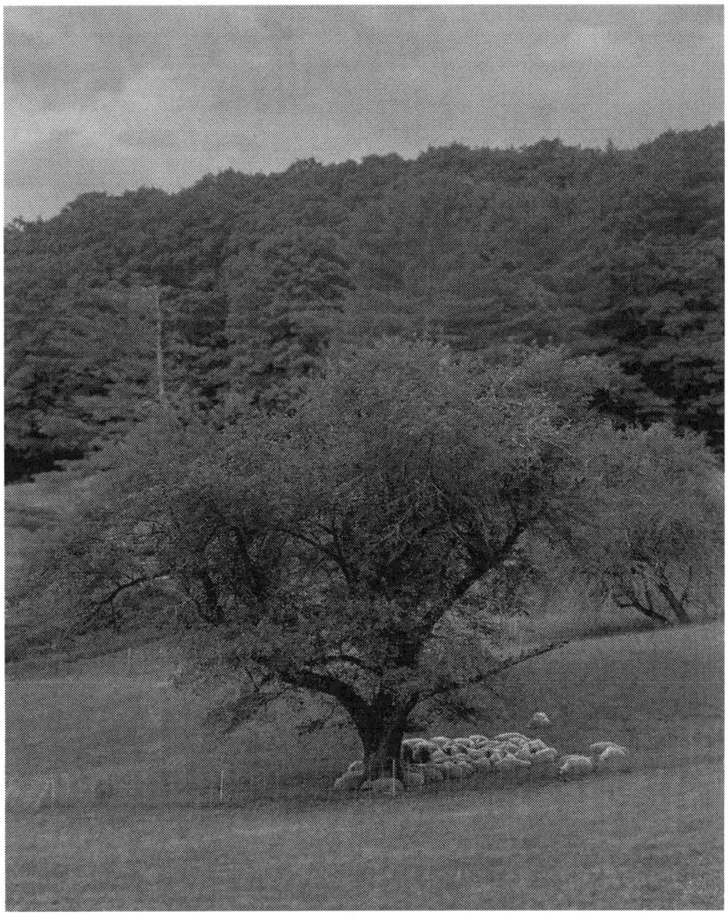

Out canoeing last night
With one of the men
Who borrowed my heart this summer

The cascading waterfalls took us through
Two rivers
Underneath a train
Past the chickens & hens
To view a startling peach
Sunset in the direction
We were flowing.

Yet under the same sky (like some kind of miracle)
A full rainbow sat above us
(We were the treasure it kept hidden in the end)

As the rain kissed our heads lightly
I couldn't stop smiling.

The Universe not only gifted us this moment,
But each other, too.

-*it's over but lovely*

I walk in the shady forest
Of black birch

Crossing the
Old stone wall
Passing through
The bursting hydrangea bushes.

Admiring the sun lit
Green maple leaves
Spread out, a canopy
Covering most of the
Baby blue sky.

Scents of lilac
And dewy sweet grass
Fill the air.
Purple thistle of red clover
Tickles my legs.

The yellow finch
Circles all around me.

I've dreamt of this.

-where she longs to be

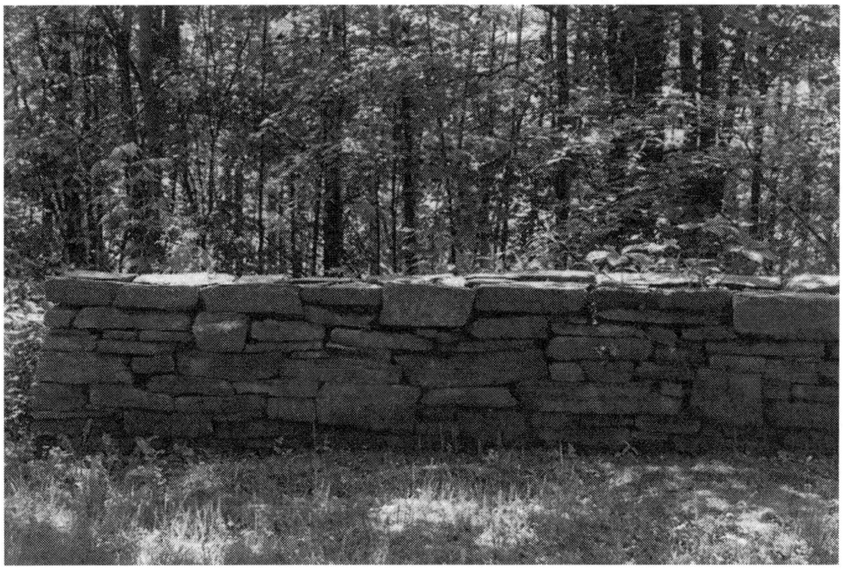

I am unbound to any lifestyle.

When the wind fluctuates,
I can turn with it.
My ability to adapt is embellished with
My willingness to welcome Change
As an old friend.

While trying at times,
I know this companion suits me best.

-a woman leaning in

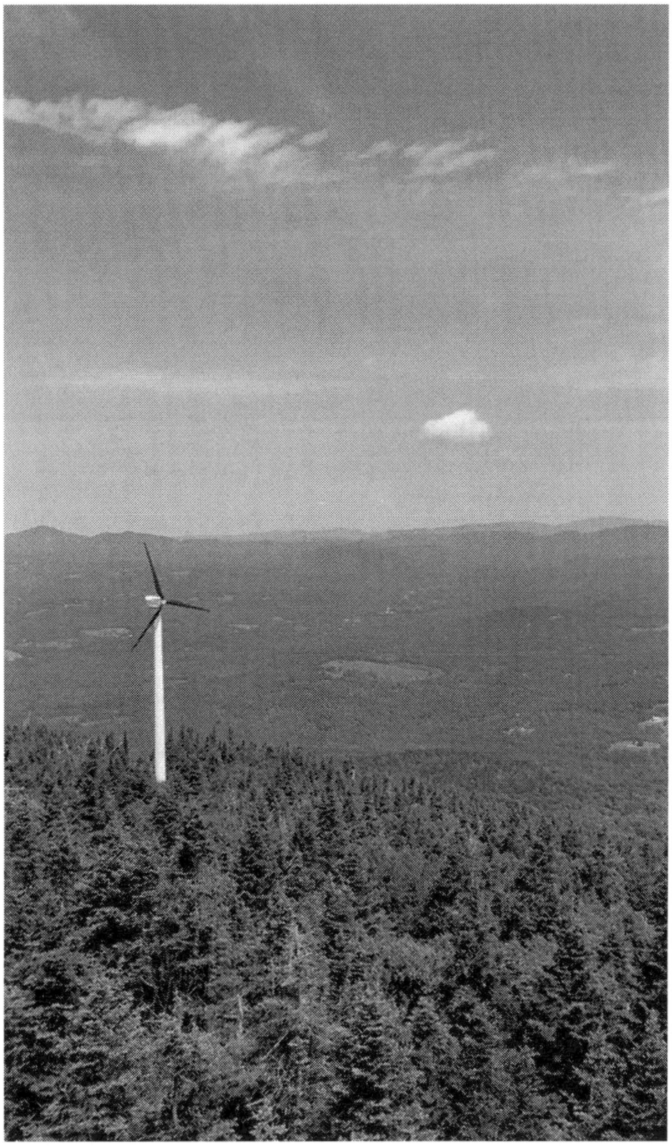

I wish I had
A witness

To everything that I've
Seen and felt
And lived through this
Little while.

Someone to look at,
And nod at me,
With a hidden smile
In their eyes
That says "I see you, and it's been a wild ride."

-a profound experience

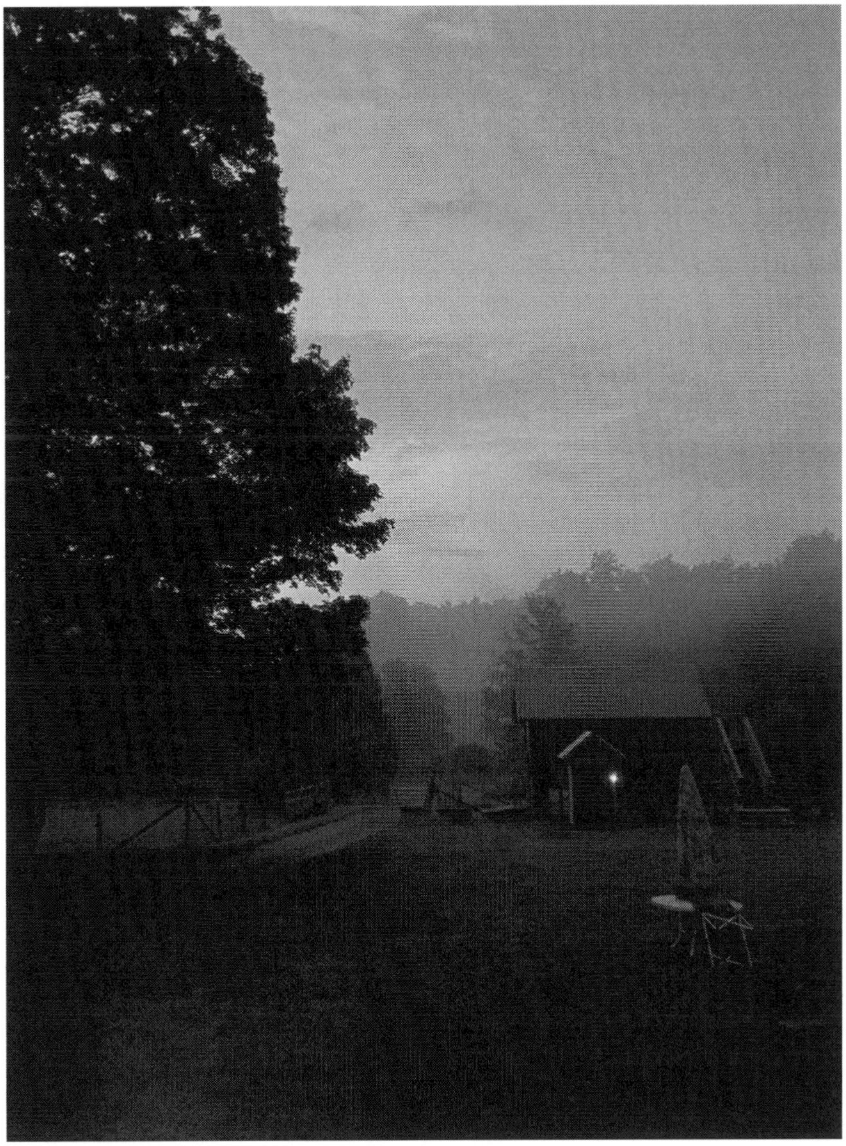

Swimming at the nude beach
In my favorite lake
Was one of those experiences
That make life's grievances worth bearing
No one was there but me
And the old man (who is always there)
Stacking rocks and lighting incense
I established myself
On the furthest beach from the trail
And set out in the frigid water
My nude physique
Tan against the backdrop
Of grey sky and pale blue waters
It began to rain, a downpour,
Enveloping all around me
As I was shoulder deep
Breathing through
The arctic chills
My hair and face
Quickly drenched
Like the rest of my body
Head tilted to the sky
Arms up overhead
Smiling expressive gratitude
Before I plunged
Into the clear,
Bubbly water all around me
Languorously swimming
Back and forth
Watching the trees uproot
The red maple leaves fall
And enjoying
The serendipity of the day.

-*an uninhibited woman*

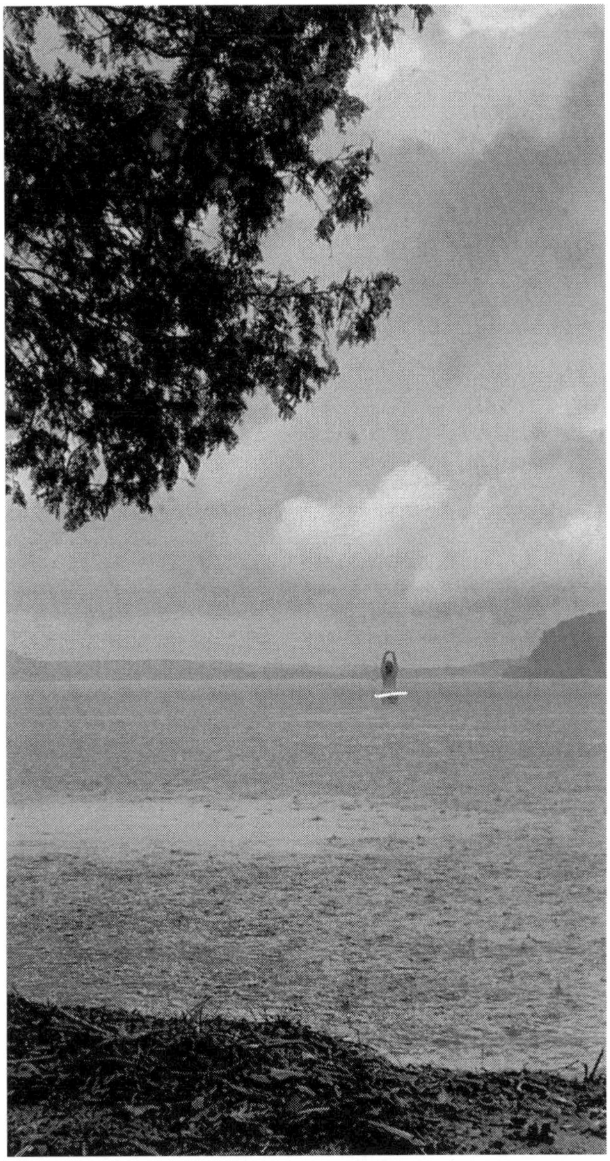

Bittersweet

How we are able
To appreciate
Something
Someone
A tender moment
That much more
When we know it's temporary.

-something to consider changing

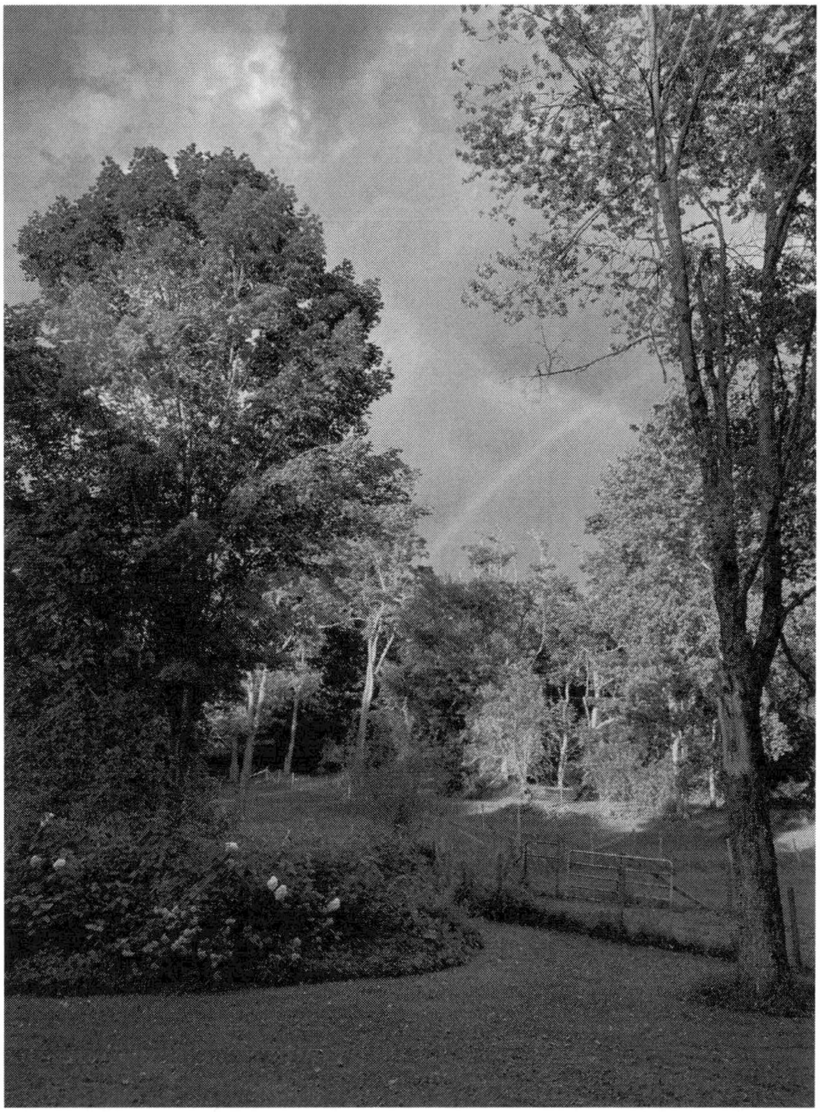

He loved me wild

He let me be free

He said I made his world more vibrant

& that an Angel, is what he thinks of me.

He wished my roaming well,
And sent me away from his arms
With the most tender kiss
A piece of his heart,
& a longing that he was joining me.

-a goodbye

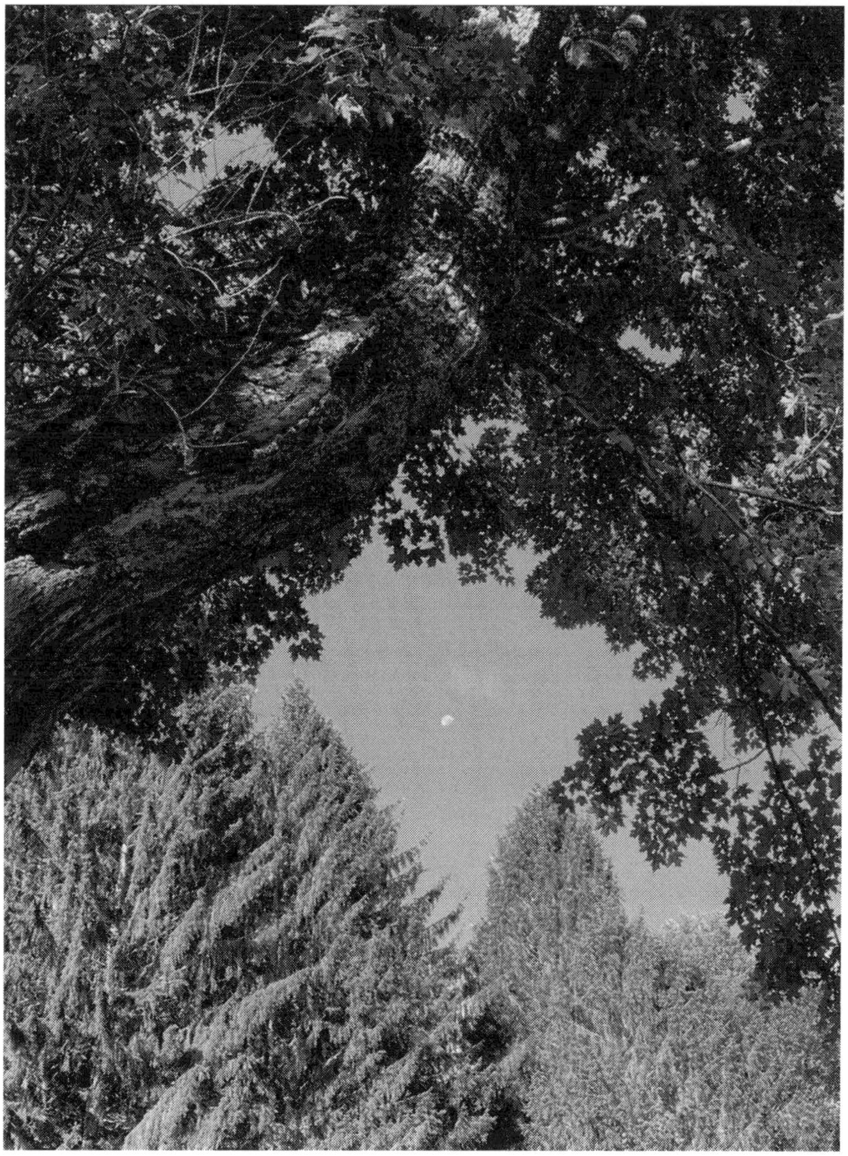

Honey girl
Full of
Wild fire

She knows who she is
And what she brings

To every interaction
And new place

If you're lucky enough
To be loved by her,
Won't you take her up
In your arms
Look into her eyes
And tell her she's beautiful?

-willing you won't

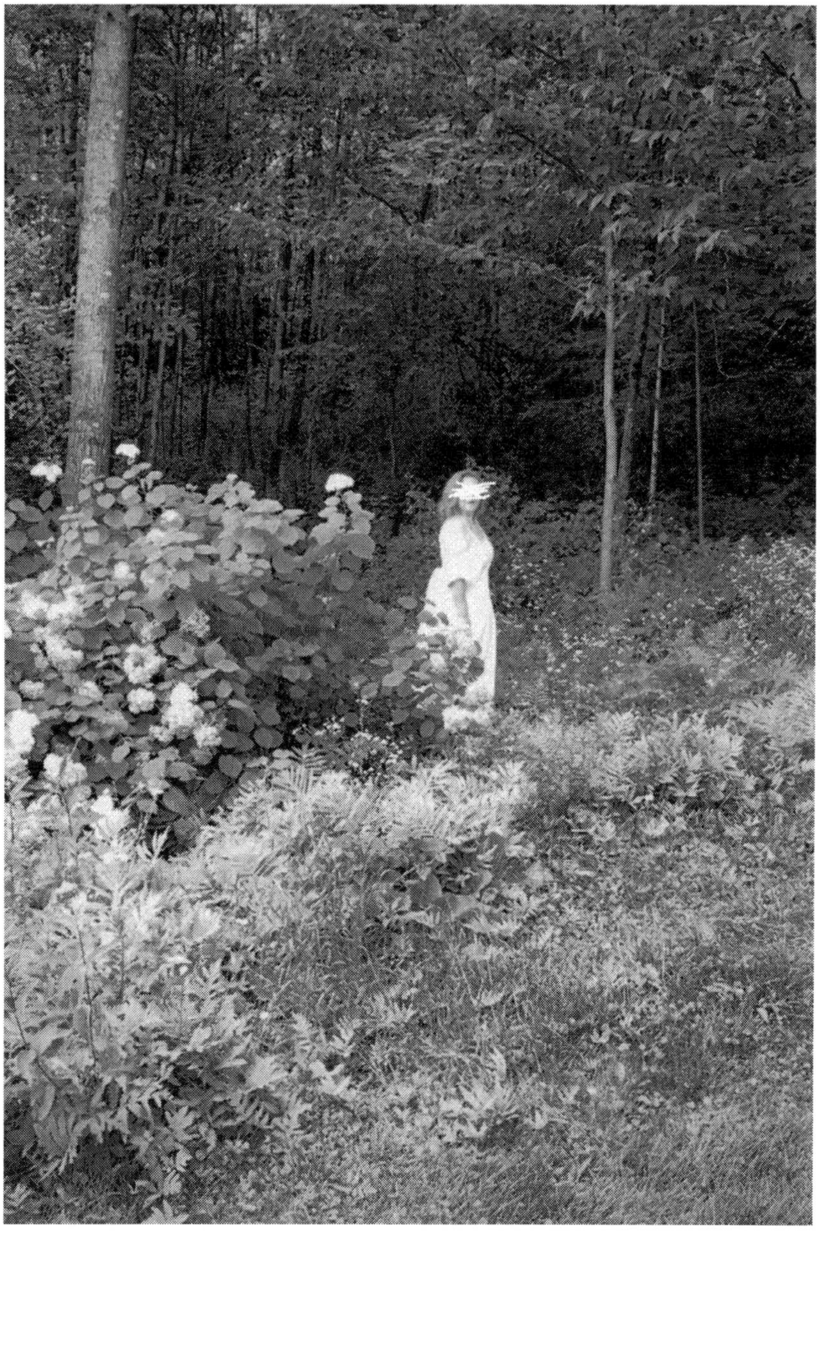

The dewey trees are breathing well this morning
Bathing in mist and sunshine
I put my hands under the waterfall to feel its power
Then cup the water over my head
I want to be a part of you, of this world around me

-the nature in me, is also in you

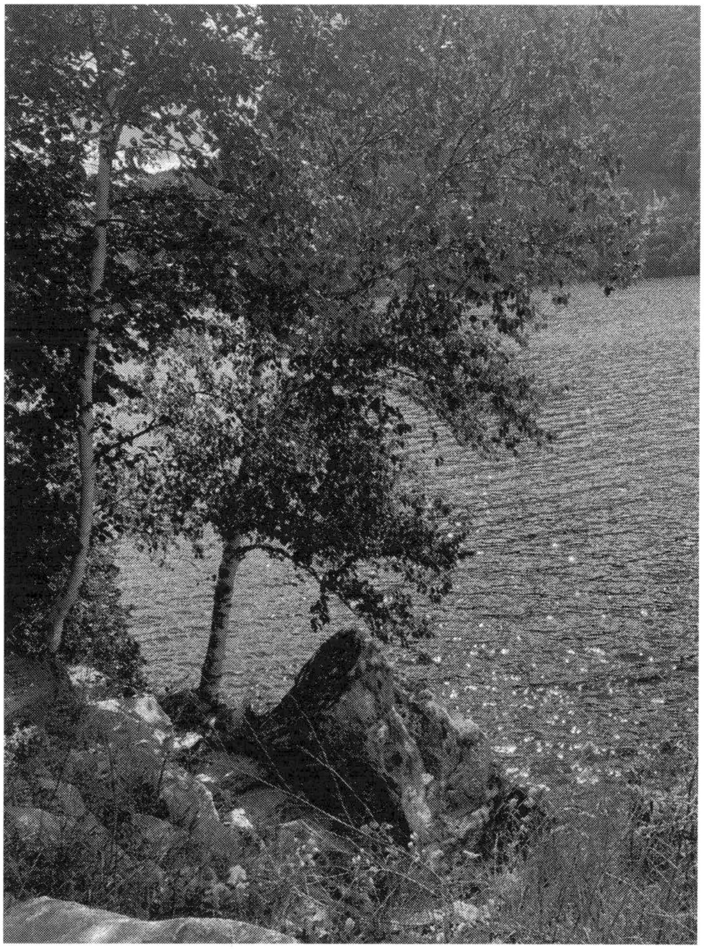

That time is over now.
We are on the other side.

Crying, I'm driving away
From here.
        From you.
A queasy pit
In my belly
And a sore in my chest.

One of my heart strings
Is tethered there now,
The heartland is weighted by this new anchor.

A fragment of your memory is knotted to mine
Somewhere dangling there, in space & time.
Will a part of you not wait for me, too?

-rose-colored memories

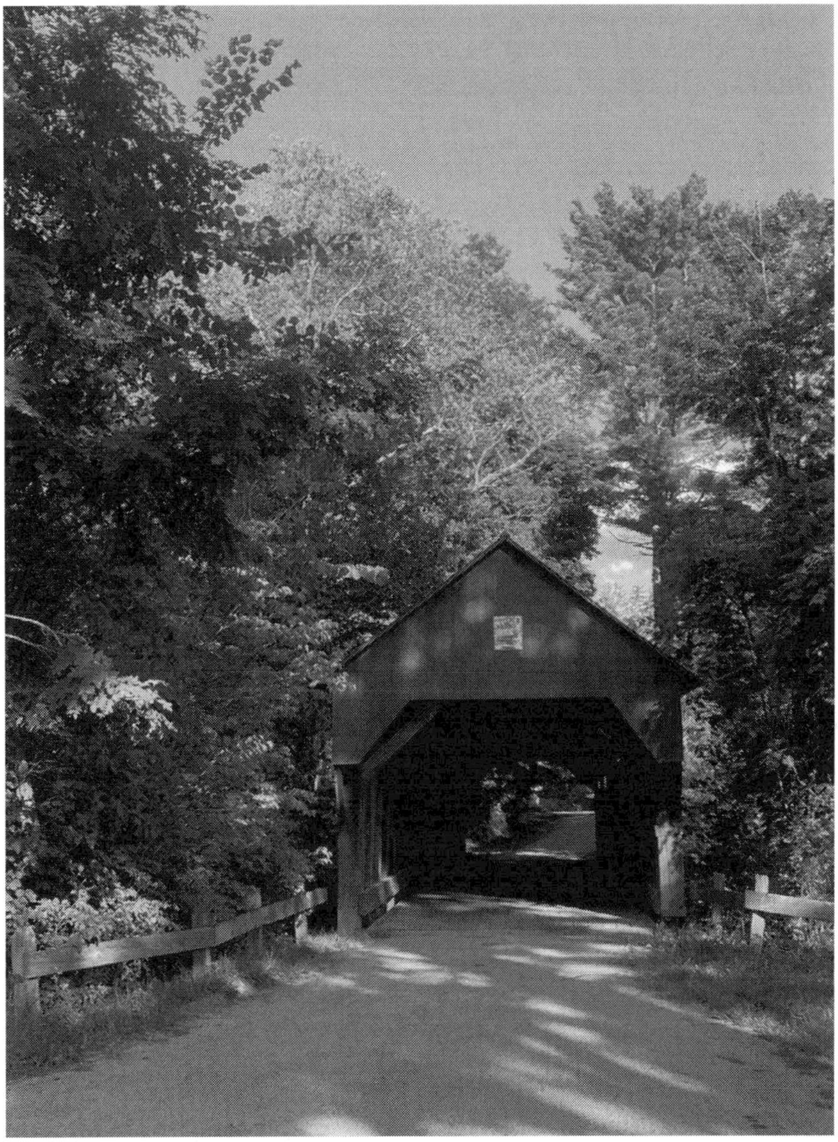

Meet me
In the woods
On the edge
Of the wide river stream
With a smile
An open hand
Or flowers

My hair all around me,
While wading in the ferns
Looking through stones

Heart as open as the sky,

Meet me
Under the cooling
Overhangs of
The pine tree
On that peak
Overlooking the towns over & beyond

Where the Adirondack chairs wait for us.

-a joining

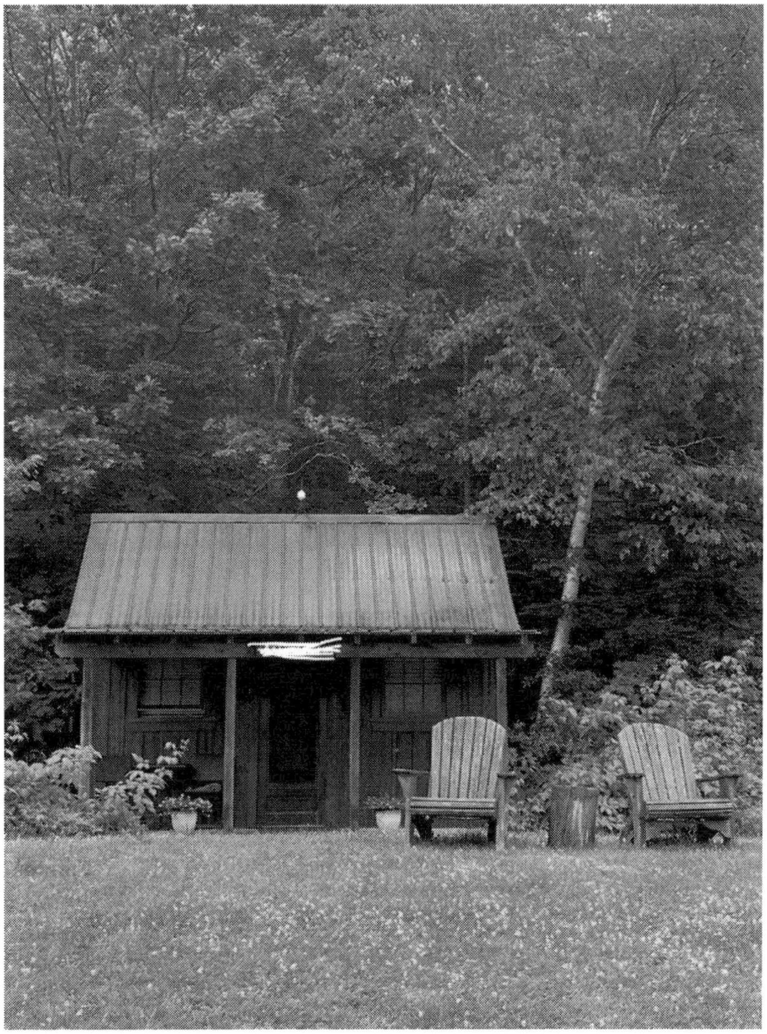

In the Green Mountains
She found the happiness she held inside
Her adoring heart

Reflected at her

She danced on the earth, near the open flame
She swam unclothed in its rivers

Open-mouthed, laughing under the stars

Presenting grace to all that she had met
Forging new friendships, lasting comraderies
Sharing, exploring her body with delightful men

Learning to hold & hand out even more love

Here, she had found a home

-mirrors from the inner world

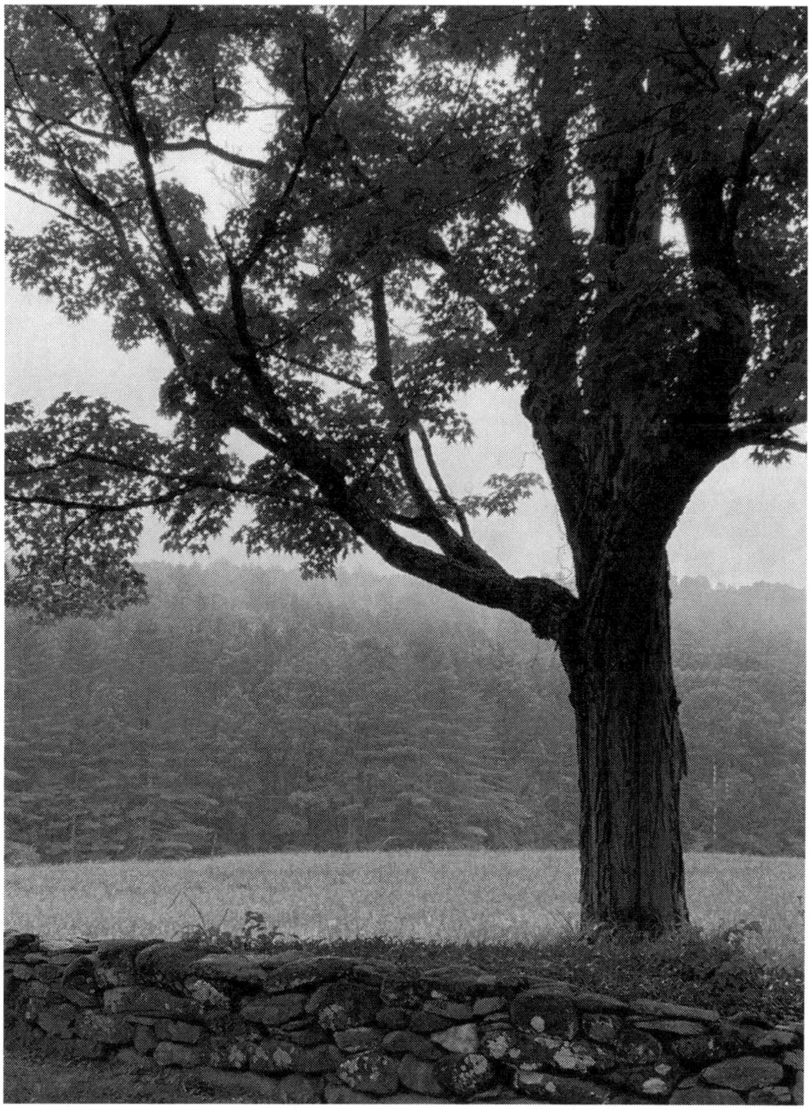

When you depart from a place
There is a touch of regret
No matter if you are longing for
Where you are headed

Because innately your bones know
Once you are gone
It will never again
Be just like this.
Captured so perfectly
In harmony.

This doesn't mean that if you come back
 It will not be great,
        (or even better!)

But it will never again be
Just like this.
This very breath.
This fragile moment of tranquility.
With these seasons,
The same people
The mood
Energy
Or unassuming gifts.

-taking a leave

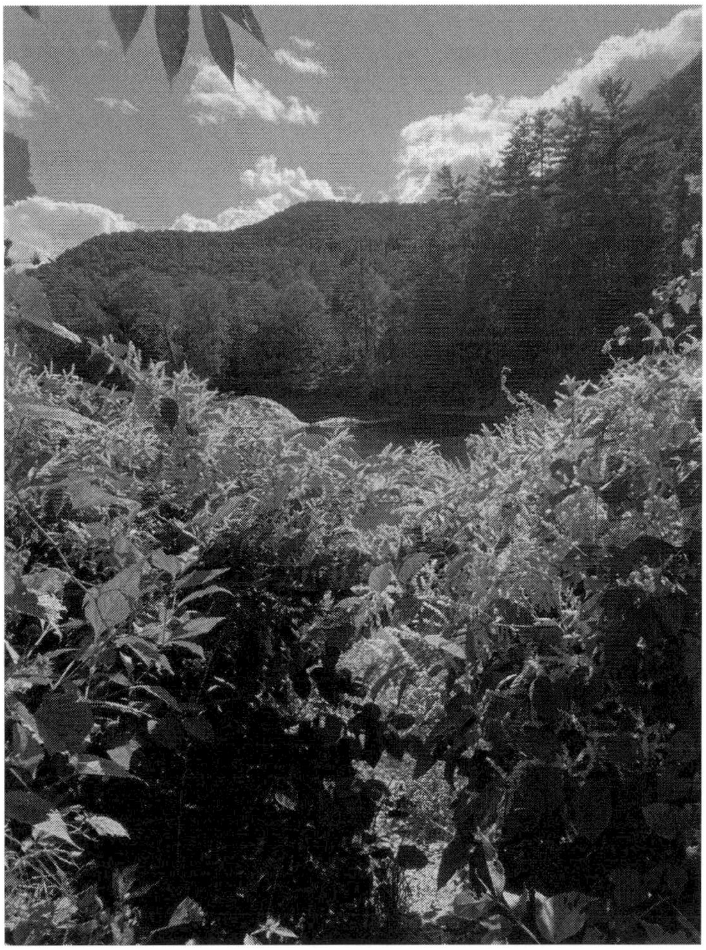

Timing
Is such a mysterious
Menacing teacher

He spun an arithmetic
Out of good potential

He made fun of
Our developing love

He exposed a lesson
Of this journey
All along

-the punishment

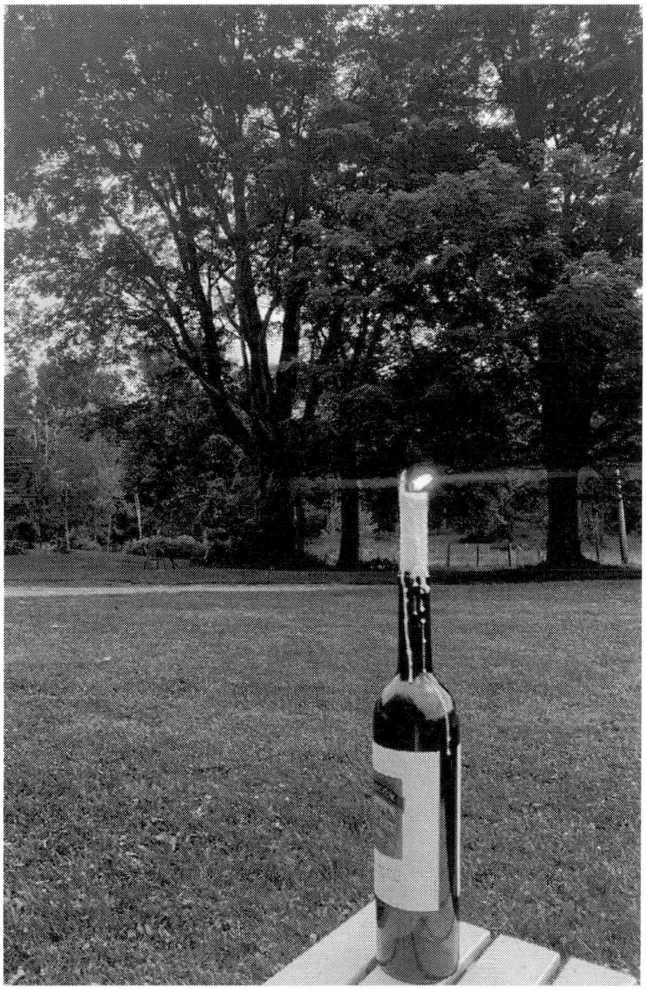

Maple syrup
Colored leaves

Friendly faces
A life of ease

I think this place was made for me.

-Vermont

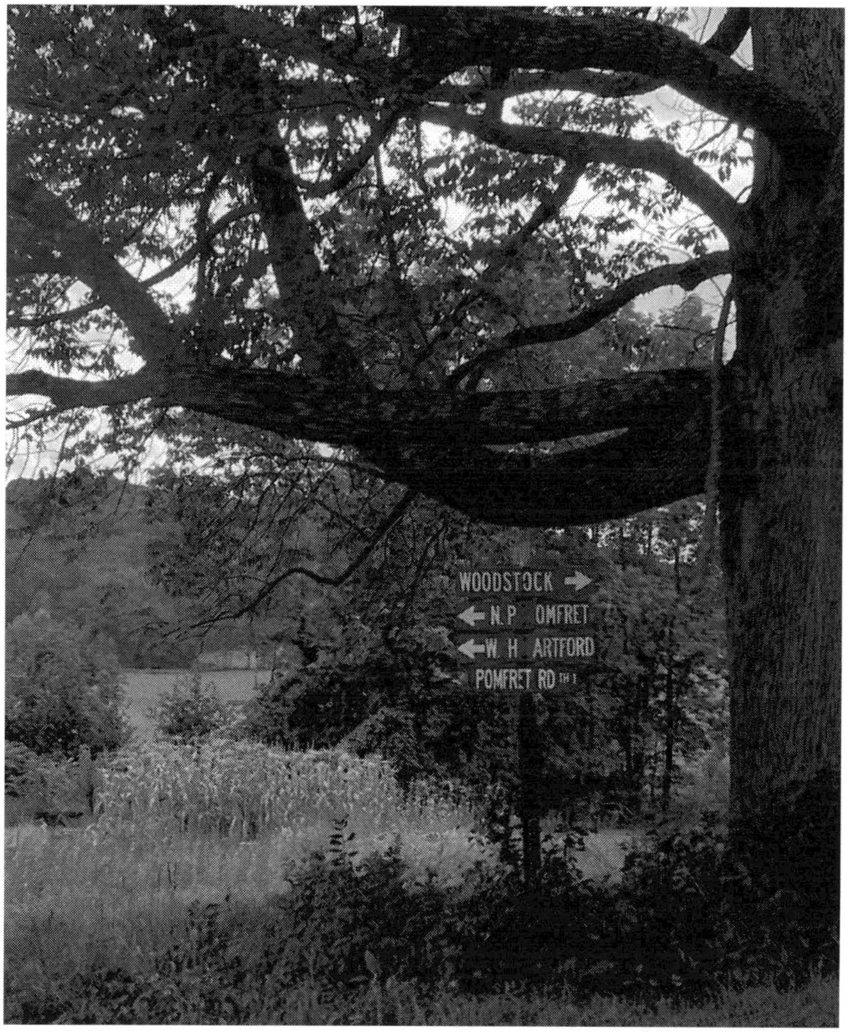
WOODSTOCK
N. P OMFRET
W. H ARTFORD
POMFRET RD

Find yourself
And then come rediscover me

Heal yourself
And I will meet you, mended

See yourself
For only the brave dare upon a closer inspection

Witness life
Let go of the past, and dream of a future

Love yourself
And then you can fearlessly love me

-later & right on time

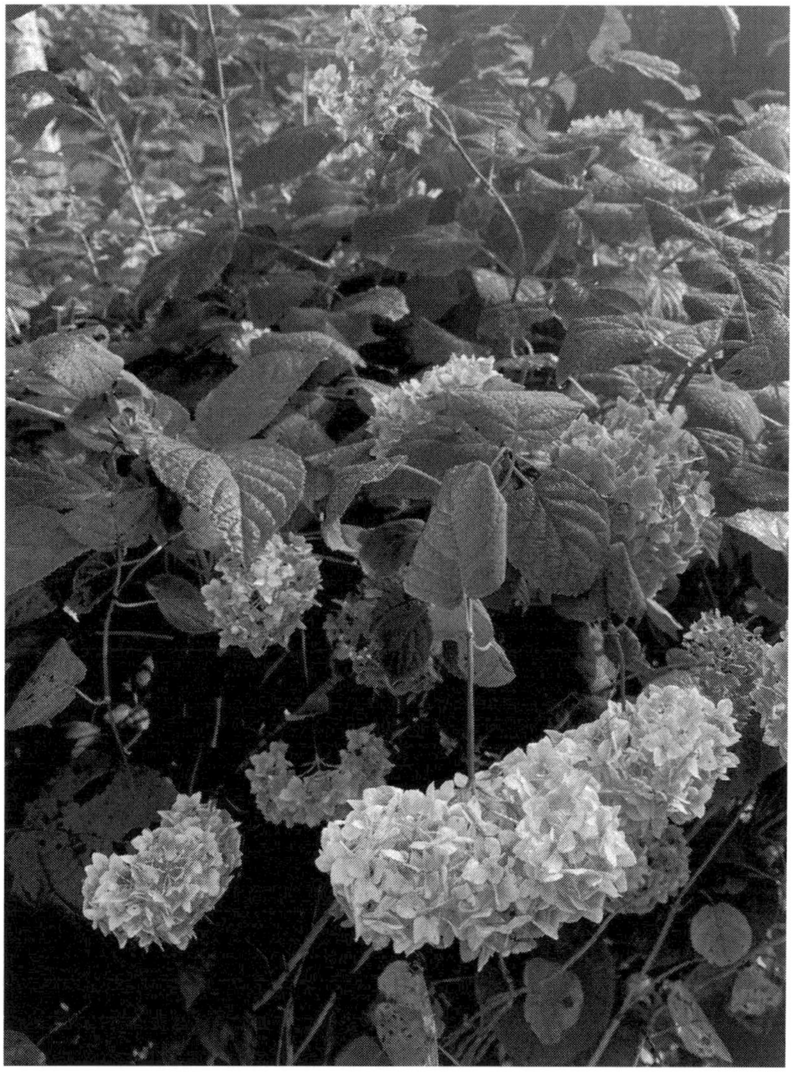

Lately each new day I've noticed
That everything green
Is turning yellow or orange
      Soon to be red.

I'm not ready
To say "goodbye" to summer
Nor "farewell" to the insects
And pastel flowers
That I admire each day

Least of all
To this place that has stolen my heart

This old farmhouse
The stone set walls
The covered bridges
And brick-built homes
Surrounded by Hemlock
And fern.

-a change begins

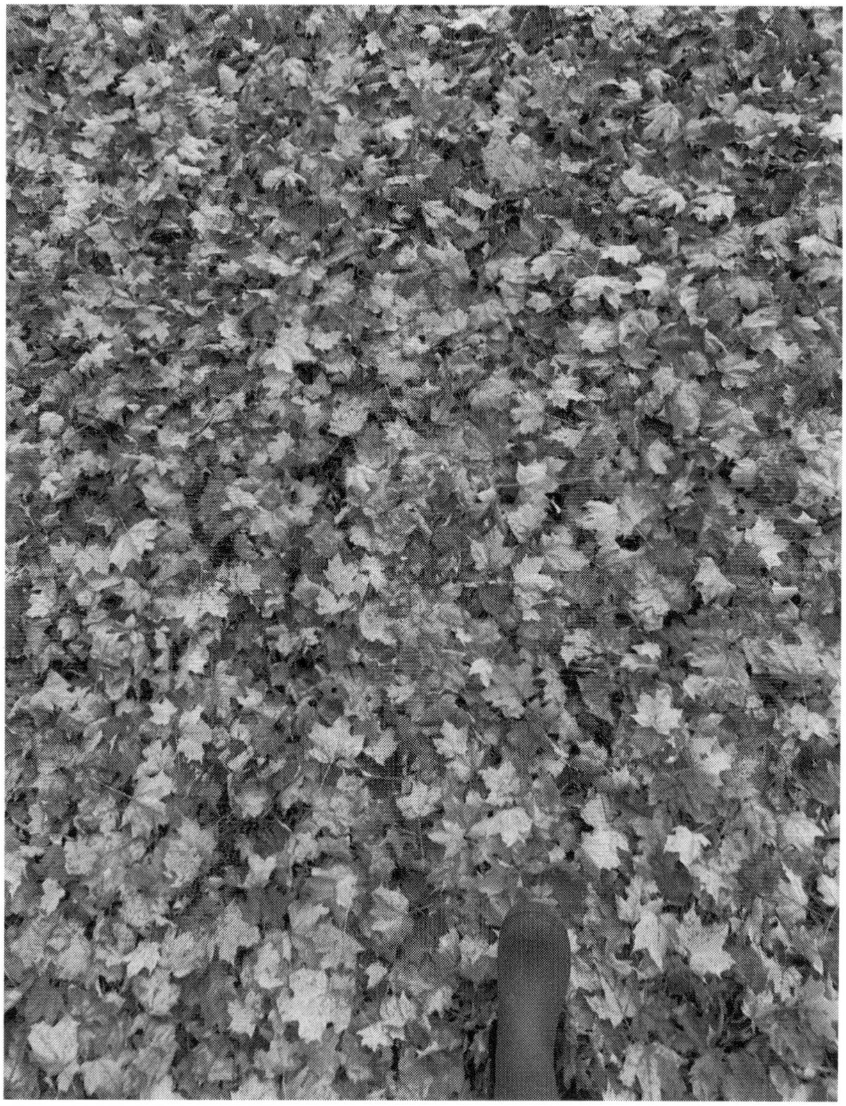

Road warrior
Cancer survivor
Mountain climber
Skinny-dipping mermaid
Earthen angel
Wild & wired

Shooting stars in my eyes
With an Artemis arrow
Right into your blazing heart

I grew up with the wolves in the West
To scurry along bear paths in the East

But the road is not laid out before me –
I create it in my wake.

-you get to choose

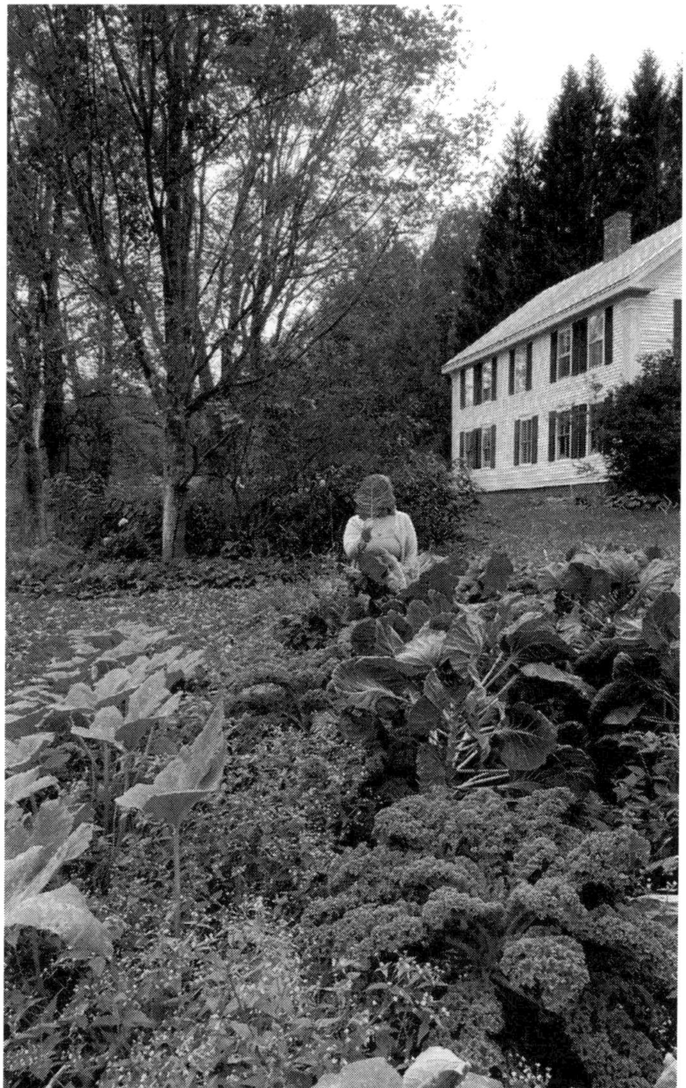

My hands are ready
And when you are
Willing

I'll gladly pour my
Cosmic heart
A sparkling, warm galaxy
Of fire and music notes

Once again
Into your waiting palm.

-the stuff of magic

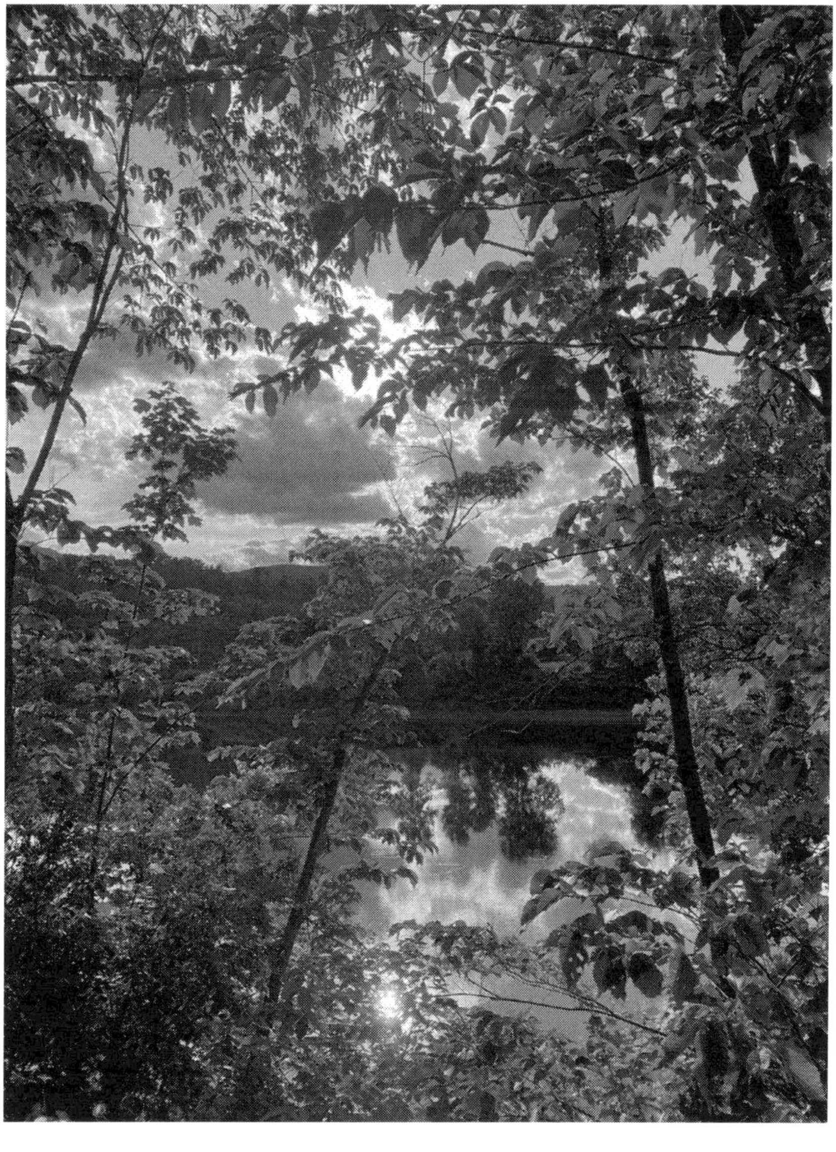

Made in the USA
Columbia, SC
04 August 2024

064ecc97-eda9-4a05-a136-28aa4e360347R01